BRANCH LINES AROUND
NORTH
WOOLWICH
from Victoria Park to Beckton and Gallions

J.E.Connor series editor Vic Mitchell

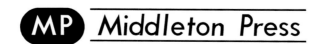

MP Middleton Press

Cover picture: Class N7 0-6-2T no. 69707 heads a North Woolwich train between Canning Town and Stratford on 25th March 1961. (A.E.Bennett)

Published March 2001

ISBN 1 901706 65 6

© Middleton Press, 2001

Cover design   Deborah Esher

Layout and typesetting London Railway Record

Published by
    Middleton Press
    Easebourne Lane
    Midhurst, West Sussex
    GU29 9AZ
Tel: 01730 813169
Fax: 01730 812601

Printed & bound by Biddles Ltd,
        Guildford and Kings Lynn

CONTENTS

INDEX

ACKNOWLEDGMENTS

Of the various lines serving the area of London now known as Docklands, the branch to North Woolwich has perhaps fared the best with photographers. It remained steam-worked into the early 1960s, and this fact no doubt tempted a number of enthusiasts on to the route.

I would therefore like to thank all those whose views fill the pages of this album, particularly Mr A.E. Bennett, who not only photograph trains, but recorded their surroundings and took a number of excellent pictures of the line in the 1950s.

GEOGRAPHICAL SETTING

The lines are on the northern flood plain of the River Thames and are situated between two of its tributaries, the River Roding and Bow Creek, except Victoria Park and Blackwall Goods Depot which are west of the latter. The line to that depot is shown south of Canning Town station. All maps are to the scale of 25 inches to 1 mile, unless stated otherwise. Bacon's map of about 1910 is below and is scaled at 1 in to 1 mile. The three termini are lower right.

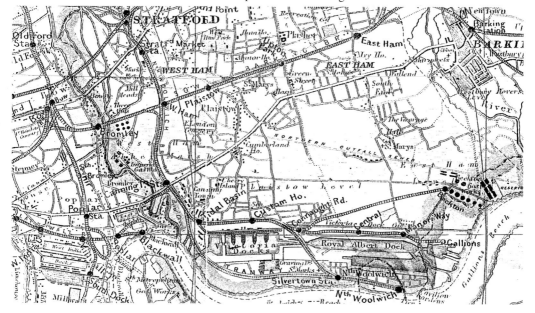

THE NORTH WOOLWICH BRANCH

The earliest section of the North Woolwich branch owed its origins to The Eastern Counties & Thames Junction Railway, which received Parliamentary Authority in July 1844. This was to commence from a junction with the Eastern Counties Railway at Stratford and extend for around 2.75 miles to Thames Wharf, near Bow Creek. Amongst its promoters was George Parker Bidder, who, together with George and Robert Stephenson, had been responsible for the construction of the nearby London & Blackwall Railway, which opened four years earlier. In the EC&TJR scheme, Bidder was joined by a few of his friends and acquaintances, including railway entrepreneurs, Peto, Brassey and Kennard. Their idea was to provide a line which would enable seaborne coal to travel from the Thames direct to East Anglia by way of the Eastern Counties Railway. However, the larger company had no

intention of building it themselves, so Bidder and his colleagues decided to press on without them.

The following year, 1845, saw the passing of an Act which authorised the North Woolwich Railway. This was to extend the EC&TJR beyond Thames Wharf and terminate on the north bank of the river, opposite the Kentish market and military town of Woolwich.

Construction of the EC&TJR was hampered by flooding around Bow Creek and Plaistow Marshes, but it eventually opened as a single line for freight traffic on 29th April 1846. A further Act, which was passed that year, permitted construction of a branch across the river Lea to the East India Dock Company's pepper warehouses at Blackwall, together with a connecting curve at Stratford, which would enable through running to and from central London. In August 1846, the Eastern Counties Railway purchased the EC&TJR and the following year also

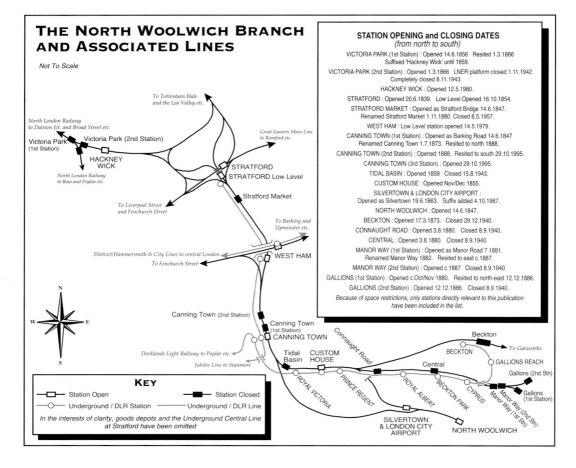

THE NORTH WOOLWICH BRANCH AND ASSOCIATED LINES

Not To Scale

STATION OPENING and CLOSING DATES
(from north to south)

VICTORIA PARK (1st Station) : Opened 14.6.1856   Resited 1.3.1866
Suffixed 'Hackney Wick' until 1859.
VICTORIA PARK (2nd Station) : Opened 1.3.1866   LNER platform closed 1.11.1942.
Completely closed 8.11.1943.
HACKNEY WICK : Opened 12.5.1980.
STRATFORD : Opened 20.6.1839.   Low Level Opened 16.10.1854.
STRATFORD MARKET : Opened as Stratford Bridge 14.6.1847.
Renamed Stratford Market 1.11.1880. Closed 6.5.1957.
WEST HAM : Low Level station opened 14.5.1979.
CANNING TOWN (1st Station) : Opened as Barking Road 14.6.1847
Renamed Canning Town 1.7.1873. Resited to north 1888.
CANNING TOWN (2nd Station) : Opened 1888. Resited to south 29.10.1995.
CANNING TOWN (3rd Station) : Opened 29.10.1995.
TIDAL BASIN : Opened 1858   Closed 15.8.1943.
CUSTOM HOUSE : Opened Nov/Dec 1855.
SILVERTOWN & LONDON CITY AIRPORT :
Opened as Silvertown 19.6.1863. Suffix added 4.10.1987.
NORTH WOOLWICH : Opened 14.6.1847.
BECKTON : Opened 17.3.1873. Closed 29.12.1940.
CONNAUGHT ROAD : Opened 3.8.1880. Closed 8.9.1940.
CENTRAL : Opened 3.8.1880. Closed 8.9.1940.
MANOR WAY (1st Station) : Opened as Manor Road 7.1881.
Renamed Manor Way 1882. Resited to east c.1887.
MANOR WAY (2nd Station) : Opened c.1887 Closed 8.9.1940.
GALLIONS (1st Station) : Opened c.Oct/Nov 1880. Resited to north-east 12.12.1886.
GALLIONS (2nd Station) : Opened 12.12.1886. Closed 8.9.1940.
*Because of space restrictions, only stations directly relevant to this publication
have been included in the list.*

North London Railway
to Dalston Jct. and Broad Street etc.

To Tottenham Hale
and the Lea Valley etc.

Victoria Park (1st Station)
Victoria Park (2nd Station)

Great Eastern Main Line
to Romford etc.

HACKNEY WICK

North London Railway
to Bow and Poplar etc.

STRATFORD
STRATFORD Low Level

Stratford Market

To Liverpool Street
and Fenchurch Street

To Barking and
Upminster etc.

District/Hammersmith & City Lines to central London
To Fenchurch Street

WEST HAM

N
W   E
S

Canning Town (2nd Station)

Canning Town
(1st Station)
CANNING TOWN

Connaught Road

Beckton

Docklands Light Railway to Poplar etc.

Jubilee Line to Stanmore

Tidal
Basin   CUSTOM
HOUSE

BECKTON

To Gasworks

Central

GALLIONS REACH

Gallions (2nd Stn)

ROYAL VICTORIA

PRINCE REGENT

ROYAL ALBERT

BECKTON PARK

CYPRUS

Manor Way (2nd Stn)
Manor Way (1st Stn)

Gallions
(1st Station)

SILVERTOWN
& LONDON CITY
AIRPORT

NORTH WOOLWICH

KEY

☐— Station Open   ■— Station Closed

○— Underground / DLR Station   — Underground / DLR Line

*In the interests of clarity, goods depots and the Underground Central Line
at Stratford have been omitted*

acquired the North Woolwich company.

On 14th June 1847, the extension to North Woolwich was opened and passenger services were introduced over the whole route which became double-track throughout two months later. For a while, much of the surrounding area remained undeveloped and in his 1847 publication *Summer Evening Rambles Round Woolwich*, the writer R. Ruegg stated *"It is singular to hear the whistle of the locomotive and the clatter of iron wheels, where twelve months since, the heron, the plover and the bittern roamed in almost undisturbed solitude."*

The Eastern Counties Railway introduced a regular service from Shoreditch to North Woolwich, where connections were made with ferries. These were operated by the ECR and carried passengers across the Thames to a pier referred to as 'South Woolwich'. This was also owned by the company and had a ticket office which offered a comprehensive range of bookings to various destinations served by the railway. Two ferries were initially employed, but in later years a further vessel was added. This traffic suffered an early set-back in 1849, when the South Eastern Railway introduced a direct service linking London with Woolwich and Gravesend.

Originally there were only two intermediate stations, and these adjoined major thoroughfares. They were named Stratford Bridge and Barking Road and opened with the line in June 1847. Stratford Bridge catered for passenger traffic only, but Barking Road and the terminus at North Woolwich both had facilities for handling freight as well. A goods depot was also situated at Thames Wharf and another opened at Blackwall a year later. This was served by the short branch authorised in 1846 and dealt with East India Dock traffic. Its layout featured a 1 in 30 climb and tight curves, which restricted the size of locomotives used for shunting.

To help compensate for the loss of traffic brought about by the South Eastern Railway's direct link to Woolwich, the ECR opened the Royal Pavilion Gardens opposite the branch terminus in 1851.

Industrial and residential developments along the branch soon followed its opening and passenger services were improved accordingly.

In 1862, the ECR merged with various smaller companies and formed the Great Eastern Railway. By this time there was a large volume of traffic using the branch and the section between Stratford Bridge and Tidal Basin was subsequently widened. The entire stretch was not tackled at once however, but carried out piecemeal between 1860 and 1892. After this, passenger trains were routed over the tracks on the east side of the formation, whilst freight trains used those to the west.

From March 1889, the London County Council began to provide free ferries across the Thames at Woolwich and attracted passengers away from the Great Eastern Railway, which charged a penny for each journey. Nevertheless, the service operated by the GER survived for a few more years and was not withdrawn until 1st October 1908.

After World War 1, the nation's railway network was largely in a very run down condition, so the majority of companies were amalgamated to form four large groups. The grouping officially took effect from 1st January 1923 and the GER was absorbed into the new London & North Eastern Railway.

Like many of London's inner-suburban branches, the route serving North Woolwich later suffered from road competition and passenger traffic declined. In the summer of 1937, trolleybuses were introduced between Stratford and the Royal Docks, and these paralleled the line for its entire length. The trains continued to run however, although services were severely disrupted by enemy action during World War ll.

As with the earlier conflict, the railway system had suffered badly, both physically and financially, so from 1st January 1948 the system was nationalised and the LNER became part of the Eastern Region of British Railways.

Passenger numbers continued to fall during the 1950s and 60s, whilst the same period witnessed the loss of freight traffic to road hauliers. After 25th August 1969, all passenger traffic east of Custom House travelled on the former down line, leaving the other track for the surviving freight trains.

In February 1978, the Chairman of the British Railways Board announced a scheme which would benefit the branch and provide it with a better service. Trains from North Woolwich were to be extended beyond Stratford Low Level, where they had previously terminated, and routed onto the North London Line by way of Victoria Park. Before these could commence however, various track alterations had to be carried out and services were suspended for a few days in September 1978. The stations were all targeted for reconstruction, although the main building at North Woolwich was retained and later restored for use as a railway museum.

The new service commenced on 14th May 1979, when an island platform was brought into use at West Ham to provided interchange facilities with the London Transport District Line station above.

At first, the service was operated by two-car diesel multiple units, but third rail electrification was introduced in 1985 and ex-Southern Region electric stock began to appear.

In 1986, operation of the branch passed to Network SouthEast and three years later it officially became part of 'North London Railways' as a prelude to privatisation.

Since then, the Docklands Light Railway Beckton route has been constructed alongside the formation between Canning Town and Custom House, whilst the tracks between Stratford and Canning Town now have the Jubilee Line alongside. Dates for these changes may be found within the photographic section of this album.

Following privatisation, the line became part of the network operated by Silverlink Train Services Ltd.

THE NORTH LONDON CONNECTION

On 15th August 1854, the Eastern Counties Railway opened a line linking Stratford with what later became Victoria Park Junction on the North London Railway Poplar branch. At first it was only used by occasional trains, but a regular passenger service was introduced two months later on 16th October. The route also proved useful for freight traffic and soon became very busy. In 1856 the NLR constructed a station to the west of the junction and named it Victoria Park & Hackney Wick.

This soon proved inadequate and was replaced by a larger station to its east in 1866, but although well patronised in its heyday, changing fortunes resulted in its closure during World War ll. Services on the line from Stratford were drastically reduced and finally withdrawn in 1942. Victoria Park station remained open for a while, but with its interchange potential gone, it attracted even less custom than before and closed completely from 8th November 1943.

Freight traffic continued however and the number of trains eventually eclipsed those using the route to Poplar. These became less as more and more traffic succumbed to road competition, but the number of workings still remained healthy.

Passenger services were restored between Dalston Western Junction and Stratford in 1979 and a new station, named Hackney Wick, was subsequently opened to the east of the erstwhile Victoria Park site.

The junction points at Victoria Park were removed on Sunday 5th May 1984 and the remaining trackwork on the Poplar branch was subsequently lifted, although a section of the route was eventually rebuilt to serve the Docklands Light Railway.

The line through Hackney Wick was electrified the following year and continues to serve an important role as part of today's North London Line.

THE ROYAL DOCKS

Whilst the North Woolwich line was still under construction, George Parker Bidder and his associates bought up all the land between Bow Creek and Gallions Reach. In 1850 and 1853, Parliamentary Authority was given for a large section of this to be developed as the Victoria Dock and construction was soon under way.

The entrance from the Thames cut through the formation of the branch and therefore necessitated the construction of a swing bridge. However, the frequent operation of this would cause serious delays to railway traffic, so it was decided to construct a new route north of the original at the expense of the dock company. This was used by all regular services, but the earlier alignment was retained for local goods workings and became colloquially known as the Silvertown Tramway, although its official title was 'The Woolwich Abandoned Line'.

The Victoria Dock was the first railway connected dock in London and was opened by HRH Prince Albert on 26th November 1855. It was located seven miles downstream from London Bridge and received a "Royal" prefix to its name in 1880.

Another realignment of the North Woolwich branch proved necessary when the neighbouring Royal Albert Dock was authorised in 1875. This was to be connected to the Victoria Dock by means of a short channel and would again require the construction of a swing bridge. Once more this was thought to be a hindrance to services, so a cut and cover tunnel was built below the level of the channel and duly brought into use. The majority of the earlier route was transferred to the dock authorities, although the Great Eastern Railway and its successors retained running powers in the event of the tunnel being temporarily unsuitable for traffic.

The new docks were built by the London & St Katharine's Dock Company and were intended for ships with a greater draught than could be accommodated at the Victoria Dock.

The Royal Albert Dock was to be illuminated by electricity from the outset and four generating stations, each equipped with a 20hp stationary steam engine, were provided for the purpose. The lighting was installed by Messrs Siemens Bros. but this was not ready in time for the official opening on 24th June 1880, which was conducted by the Duke and Duchess of Connaught.

The last of the Royal group to be built was the King George V Dock, which opened on 8th July 1921. This adjoined the south side of the Royal Albert Dock and contained a water area of sixty-four acres, served by over three miles of quays.

GALLIONS BRANCH

The Act which authorised the construction of the Royal Albert Dock also included powers for the company to build a *"Passenger and Parcels Railway"*, therefore providing a means for staff to get to and from their place of work, and to a lesser extent, ships' passengers to reach the berths.

The line was to commence at Albert Dock Junction, 34 chains to the east of Custom House station on the North Woolwich line and extend for a distance of 1 mile 61 chains to a riverside terminus at Gallions Reach. Three intermediate stations were planned and these were clearly intended to be used by the workforce. The authorising Act stipulated that trains had to operate every day *"...upon the whole length of the railway, calling at all intermediate stations, not later than 7am and not earlier than 6pm for the conveyance of artizans, mechanics and daily labourers (both male and female) at fares not exceeding one penny per passenger..."*

Work on the line was still progressing at the time of the dock opening, so trains did not commence operating until 3rd August 1880. At first the service only ran between Custom House and Central, but by the autumn of the same year, it was extended to Gallions.

Although planned as double track, the formation was initially single with run-round loops at either end.

According to the majority of published works, the service to Gallions commenced in November 1880, but a Board of Trade report referring to an inspection made on 30th October states that the company wanted to *"...introduce the working of two trains instead of one on their branch line to Gallions Reach* (sic) *station..."* This implies that the service started earlier than previously acknowledged, but whether this was indeed the case is uncertain.

The second track as far as Central station was inspected on 14th November 1881 and opened for traffic, whilst the remaining section of double formation was brought into use on 1st April 1882.

Initially, all services were provided by the London & St Katharine's Dock Company, with, for the first few months, locomotives hired from the contractors, Lucas & Aird.

From 1st January 1889 the London & St Katharines company united with the East & West India Docks organisation under the banner of a joint committee. This remained operative for twelve years, after which the two bodies officially amalgamated and became The London & India Docks Company.

Unfortunately mergers such as this did little to improve the ailing finances of the various docks which suffered from the effects of inter-company competition. Therefore, in 1902, a Royal Commission investigating the situation reported in favour of a completely unified port management for the capital. After a great deal of discussion, a plan was eventually agreed and from 31st March 1909, all the former dock companies were absorbed into the new Port of London Authority.

For all the problems of the docks themselves, the branch line to Gallions was an unqualified success, with patronage reaching its zenith in the early years of the twentieth century. Unfortunately this prosperity was not destined to last however, and the line's fortunes began to suffer during World War 1.

The situation continued to deteriorate between the wars and public demand became less and less.

During the afternoon of 7th September 1940, referred to locally as "Black Saturday", the entire area around the docks was devastated by the first major air raid of the Blitz and the line was put out of action. The stations were closed and a substitute bus service came into operation. Although the track was later repaired to enable wagon storage, the passenger trains were never reinstated and the abandonment was officially authorised by Section 29 of the Port of London Act 1950.

Apart from the Gallions branch, the Royal Docks were also served by boat trains, which ran along the tracks normally only used for freight traffic. Some of these terminated beside transit sheds in the Royal Albert Dock, whilst others went to the King George V.

Boat trains would leave the North Woolwich line at Albert Dock Junction, where the signalman, although latterly a British Railways' employee, had half his wages paid by the PLA. From here, the BR driver would invariably have a PLA pilotman with him for the run through the dock estate.

Today, the old Gallions branch has largely disappeared, although a section of the Docklands Light Railway Beckton line closely follows part of its route. This however is constructed on a completely new trackbed and precious few relics of the earlier route remain visible.

BECKTON BRANCH

In 1867, the Gas Light & Coke Company applied for Parliamentary Authority to erect a huge new gasworks to serve London. It was to be sited on previously undeveloped marshland to the southwest of Barking Creek and built to the design of the company's chief engineer.

The premises were to be located on the bank of the Thames with a pier for the off-loading of coal for gas production. There would also be an internal railway system, intended for the transportation of fuel and waste products around the works.

The scheme met full approval and the Act received the Royal Assent the following year. The first pile in the river wall was ceremonially driven by the company's Governor, Simon Adams Beck on 29th November 1868 and the works complex was given the name Beckton in his honour.

When complete, the gasworks occupied a site of 269 acres and boasted a river frontage which stretched for almost half a mile.

The site was remote to say the least and apart from the pier, its only connection with the outside world was an unsurfaced road which linked it to Barking. Because of this, the company constructed a small colony of houses to accommodate some of its employees. The majority of these were compact cottages for the ordinary workmen and their families, but there were also a few larger houses for supervisory grades. To complete the settlement there was a Methodist chapel, recreation ground, social club and public house.

The new works were soon operative and gas was first manufactured on 25th November 1870. A few days later, on 8th December, Beckton began to supply the City by means of a 48 inch diameter main. The scheme was a total success.

The construction of a branch line linking Beckton with Custom House on the Great Eastern Railway's North Woolwich line was authorised by the Gas Light & Coke Company Act of 1871.

This was financed by the gas company and comprised a single track.

Goods traffic associated with the gas industry began operating on 14th October 1872, to be followed by a service of passenger trains for workmen on 17th March 1873.

Although built and initially worked by the Gas Light & Coke Company, the branch was leased to the Great Eastern Railway from 18th March 1874, after which the GER operated the trains.

The station at Beckton was 2 miles 1 chain from Custom House, and although regarded as a terminus, the tracks continued beyond the single platform, to connect with the internal gasworks system.

Expansion of the works of course demanded extra staff and it was not possible to accommodate all of them at Beckton. Therefore in its early years the branch from Custom House was to prove invaluable. Workmen's trains were operated, giving employees a cheap and convenient means of getting to their place of work.

The coming of electric tramways in the early part of the twentieth century gave some of the employees another means of travel. On 22nd June 1901, East Ham Corporation introduced a service to New Beckton, which was extended just under two years later to the Royal Albert Dock. In 1905 another tram route opened, this time it linked the gasworks with the centre of Barking. Perhaps these developments helped to erode some of the branch passenger traffic, but employees who lived along the Stratford line had to remain faithful to the trains, as there were no tramways linking their district with Beckton.

The situation changed however following the construction of the Barking Bypass in 1927. Buses were introduced between Stratford, Canning Town and Beckton, and people began to forsake the railway for the comparative comfort and convenience of the bus. In time, the trams also fell victim to the internal combustion engine and the last route serving Beckton, the 73 from Wanstead, was replaced by the 101 bus in October 1936.

For all this, freight traffic continued to abound, with supplies for the gasworks being taken to Beckton and wagons loaded with coke and other by-products travelling in the opposite direction.

Not surprisingly, Beckton gasworks received a great deal of damage during the London Blitz. Over this period, the premises were struck by more than 200 bombs and all of the gasholders were at some time hit.

Traffic on the branch was suspended after the first devastating attack on 7th September 1940, but was restored once necessary repairs had been carried out. However, there was no longer any demand for the passenger trains, so these were withdrawn permanently from the end of December 1940.

Nevertheless, freight services continued, and for a while, increased. With East Coast shipping lanes subject to enemy attack, some of the coal required for the works began to arrive by rail and additional reception sidings were constructed.

The end of hostilities in 1945 left much of the surrounding area as a devastated ruin, but Beckton gasworks survived and remained functional. The gas industry became nationalised in the post-war era and the responsibility for Beckton passed to the North Thames Gas Board.

For the first decade or so, the works continued to prosper, but by the mid 1960s, new production methods brought about its decline.

The final ship load of coal was delivered on 16th April 1969 and two months later, on 16th June, coal gas manufacture at Beckton ceased completely.

At 17.15 on 1st June 1970, the last ever working from Beckton, a load of pitch from the By-Products Works, set off on its journey. Although devoid of traffic, the branch remained technically open until February 1971 and by early 1973, its track had been lifted.

PASSENGER SERVICES

NORTH WOOLWICH BRANCH

The initial 1847 ECR service from Shoreditch to North Woolwich operated hourly, but this was later increased to half-hourly. In June 1854, the number of trains was again increased with the introduction of workings to and from Fenchurch Street. These also ran every thirty minutes and operated by way of Stratford. From March 1858 however, an alternative route became available following the opening of the Abbey Mills spur near West Ham.

From 1st June 1887, a service was introduced linking North Woolwich with Palace Gates station in Wood Green. This ran through Stratford, Lea Bridge and South Tottenham, and continued until the Palace Gates branch closed in January 1963. After this, the majority of trains serving North Woolwich only operated to and from Stratford Low Level.

The earliest passenger service on the Eastern Counties Railway connection to Victoria Park comprised around two coaches, which would be coupled to the rear of North London Railway trains operating between Hampstead Road (near the later station at Primrose Hill) and Fenchurch Street. On reaching the junction these would be detached and hauled to Stratford Bridge by an engine provided by the NLR. Various methods of working were tried in the opposite direction, but attaching the additional vehicles proved problematical and occasionally dangerous. At one time they were added to the rear, but the shunting movements were time consuming, so they were later put on the front. When this was done, the locomotive which had hauled the main train from Fenchurch Street would be detached and replaced by that which had brought the two carriages from Stratford Bridge.

The difficulties eased slightly when Victoria Park & Hackney Wick station was opened to the west of the junction in 1856, but the process of attaching and detaching was still hazardous and was subsequently dispensed with from the end of December 1859.

The North London Railway withdrew its Victoria Park - Stratford Bridge service on 1st September 1866, but it was reinstated by the GER two months later. It reverted to the NLR on 1st November 1867 and the two companies continued to work it alternately for seven years. The last North London Railway train to and from Stratford ran on 31st October 1874 and after this the link was provided by the GER only.

The trains were extended to Canning Town from 1st October 1895 and ran at half-hourly intervals. By the early years of the twentieth century, the service was locally known as 'Stratford Jack', although the origins of this are unclear.

From 1st January 1917, the passenger service was cut to hourly, then reduced even more in 1921. Sunday trains were withdrawn after 7th October 1923, but a few continued operating on weekdays until they ceased altogether from 1st November 1942.

From 14th May 1979 however, the link was brought back into public use, when diesel multiple units began operating between North Woolwich and Camden Road on the North London Line. Initially these ran fast between Canonbury and Stratford, but intermediate stops were later added at Dalston Kingsland, Hackney Central, Homerton and Hackney Wick, with all but the last named being located on sites of earlier stations.

Electrification of the route east of Dalston Western Junction on 13th May 1985 allowed trains which had previously operated between Richmond and Broad Street to be diverted to North Woolwich instead.

Prior to May 1999 a basic twenty minute service was provided over the entire route, but from that date, the trains were increased to run every fifteen minutes north of Stratford, but reduced to just two an hour on the section to North Woolwich.

In the same year, Anglia Railways introduced a service linking towns on the former GER Colchester main line with Basingstoke. These travelled by way of Stratford and the North London Line, before joining the former London & South Western Railway near Kew.

GALLIONS BRANCH

On the Gallions branch, the London & St Katharine's Dock Company originally provided a service every thirty minutes to and from Custom House. This operated between the hours of 8.30am and 6pm but demand was such that the timetable had to be revised in 1881 to accommodate three trains an hour. In July of that year, the

Great Eastern Railway began to use the line and introduced hourly workings which linked Gallions with Fenchurch Street. These ran by way of Bromley and the Abbey Mills spur, and took thirty-two minutes to complete the journey. During this period, the dock company continued to operate a local service between Gallions and Custom House, comprising twenty-six up workings and twenty-four down. From 1st July 1896, the operation of these locals was taken over by the GER, although the branch continued to be dock property and was staffed by dock employees.

Business was really booming at the turn of the century, with a weekday service of sixteen through trains to Fenchurch Street and thirteen in the opposite direction. A few took the route though Bow Road and Stratford, but the majority used the Abbey Mills spur. The fastest of these completed the journey in twenty-five minutes, whilst the slowest took seven minutes longer. There were also two workings from Liverpool Street and a handful of trains which turned back at either Stratford Low Level or Stratford Market.

The Custom House locals continued to run and made seventy journeys a day. Most of these took around ten minutes and called at all stations, although a couple ran non-stop around the start and close of service, presumably for positioning purposes.

As the years progressed, the traffic declined and the service was cut back. Sunday trains were taken off from 27th June 1915 and bank holiday workings ceased three years later. At the beginning of 1918, a special service for munitions workers was operated, which ran to a jetty east of Gallions station and linked with a ferry to Woolwich Arsenal. However, with the end of hostilities this ceased to be necessary and was therefore withdrawn. The local Custom House - Gallions workings were taken off in 1932, leaving just the through trains, although by then these were reduced in number.

Following the outbreak of World War II, the decision was made to close the line after 1.10pm on Saturdays and not reopen it until 7.20am on Mondays. By this time the service had further diminished, and the total number of trains in both directions had dropped to just twenty-eight.

BECKTON BRANCH

On the other branch from Custom House, passenger trains always operated to suit the requirements of Beckton gasworks and ran at times to fit in with the shifts. Most services operated from either Stratford Low Level or Stratford Bridge and called at all stations.

A timetable including all three branches can be seen opposite pictures 56 and 57.

1. Victoria Park to North Woolwich

VICTORIA PARK

The first station at Victoria Park comprised two short platforms and was entered from the north side of Wick Road.

It was brought into use on 29th May 1856 to serve celebrations marking the end of the Crimean War, but regular traffic did not begin until a couple of weeks later on 14th June.

Originally the platforms were open to the elements, but waiting rooms and awnings were later erected. Within a decade however, the premises began to prove inadequate for the growing traffic, so the North London Railway decided to build a completely new station, south-east of the original. This was a much larger affair with a three storey building which faced onto Cadogan Terrace and overlooked the fringe of the park itself.

The new station was opened as a direct replacement for its predecessor on 1st March 1866 and was located at the junction between the diverging Poplar and Stratford routes.

There were initially four platform faces, with two on each line, but that serving the eastbound GER track proved to be little used and was demolished during August 1895.

The station continued to prosper however and an additional entrance was opened at its north-western end on 1st February 1899. This was reached by means of a covered walkway from the eastern side of Riseholme Street, but its booking hall was always referred to as the 'Hackney Wick Office' or 'Victoria Park No 2'.

By this time, the station was at its zenith, but its fortunes were soon to decline. As with so many inner-suburban routes, those serving Victoria Park were subsequently hit by bus and tram competition and passenger numbers plummeted. The Stratford service was withdrawn from 1st November 1942, then a year later, on 8th November 1943, Poplar trains ceased to call and the station was closed completely.

1. In this view from the early 1900s, a Great Eastern train has just arrived from the Stratford direction and its locomotive prepares to run-round. Even in the station's early days it seems that the majority of GER services used the westbound platform for both arriving and departing, so that serving the other track proved little used from the outset. It was sited to the left of the picture, but its demolition must have been very thorough, as no signs of it are visible here. (Charles Martin Series Postcard/J.E. Connor Collection)

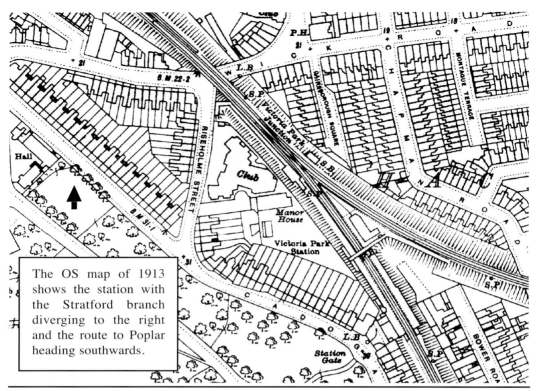

The OS map of 1913 shows the station with the Stratford branch diverging to the right and the route to Poplar heading southwards.

2. This view, taken from the north-western end of the central platform shows the Poplar branch to the left and the Stratford tracks on the right. The signal box can also be seen, but the chief point of interest is the rare glimpse of the supplementary entrance building of 1899. The rear of this appears to the left, together with the covered way which led from Riseholme Street. It closed on 29th January 1940 and had disappeared completely by 1950. (J.E. Connor Collection)

3. Apart from the loss of the Wick Road entrance and a nearby footbridge, Victoria Park remained largely intact until 1950, but within six years its condition had deteriorated drastically. This eastwards view shows the station in April 1956, with the Stratford route in the foreground and the Poplar line to the right. The latter retained short sections of platform awning over its stairwells, but the former GE side was looking very desolate. Demolition of the brick building on the central platform started in the Spring of 1959, and was probably completed soon afterwards. (L. Collings)

4. On 5th May 1956, Fowler class 3F 0-6-0T No 47517, is held on the westbound Poplar line, as No 47647 of the same class rattles across the junction with a freight from Stratford. (E.R. Wethersett)

5. This is the signal box on 12th August 1956, as viewed from a freight train taking the junction towards Stratford. Despite the loss of passenger services, both routes from Victoria Park saw a great deal of goods traffic throughout the 1950s and well into the 1960s. (A.E. Bennett)

6. The station exterior appeared little altered for many years after closure. Here it is seen in 1963, looking across Cadogan Terrace from outside the park gates. At this time, the topmost storey of the building was inhabited, but with the exception of an access door below, the rest was empty. The booking hall had been located at street level, whilst the first floor faced onto the westbound Poplar line platform. (J.S. Phillips)

7. In the early months of World War ll, a nationwide plan was implemented to remove signs from railway stations and other landmarks to confuse the enemy if they invaded. Unfortunately the only people to be confused were those going about their daily business, so in time the ban was relaxed and names began to re-appear. This 'temporary' paper sticker on one of the soot-blackened windows of the main building at track level is thought to have dated from this period and remained in ever-deteriorating condition until at least 1966. (J.E. Connor)

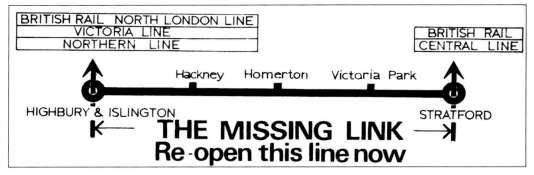

BRITISH RAIL NORTH LONDON LINE
VICTORIA LINE
NORTHERN LINE

BRITISH RAIL
CENTRAL LINE

Hackney   Homerton   Victoria Park

HIGHBURY & ISLINGTON   STRATFORD

⟵ THE MISSING LINK ⟶
Re-open this line now

During the 1950s and 60s, the occasional letter would appear in the local press questioning the wisdom of using the routes through Victoria Park for freight traffic only. At the time of closure it was thought that buses would provide a viable and more economical alternative, but as roads became progressively choked with more and more vehicles, pressure was exerted on British Rail to reopen the connection to Stratford. This sticker dates from around 1972. (J.E. Connor Collection)

8. On 14th May 1979, a service of diesel multiple units began operating between Camden Road on the North London Line and North Woolwich. At first there were no intermediate stations between Canonbury and Stratford, but four were subsequently added. This view shows an east-bound train passing the site of Victoria Park Junction, as it heads towards Stratford around 1985. The signal box dated from 1961 and replaced the earlier cabin shown in photograph No 5. Traffic on the Poplar line fell to an all-time low and by the 1970s, the formation south of Victoria Park had been singled. The junction points were removed in May 1984 and the surviving track was lifted soon after. The signal box was used for a while by the Permanent Way Department, but its upper section was later demolished following fire damage, leaving just the derelict brick base which remained standing in 2000. (D. Nelson / J.E. Connor Collection)

HACKNEY WICK

9.   The new station serving Victoria Park was not constructed on the earlier site, but a short distance to the east. Originally it was to be called Wallis Road, but by the time of opening on 12th May 1980, it was named Hackney Wick. This view, looks west towards the erstwhile Junction in 1985 and shows the conductor rails in place for the electrification which was introduced in the May of that year. (J.L. Crook)

10.   A westbound two-car diesel unit is seen from the footbridge as it enters the station on the same day. (J.L. Crook)

NORTH OF STRATFORD

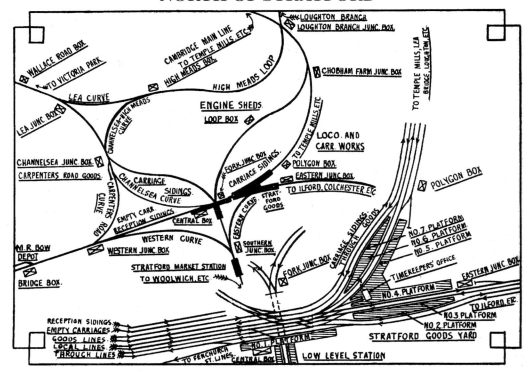

This simplified diagram, dating from 1919 clearly shows the complex of lines around Stratford and the location of signal boxes. Trains from Victoria Park would enter the map at top left and pass Wallis Road, which is incorrectly shown as 'Wallace Road'. Beyond here, they would head in a south-easterly direction at Lea Junction, then continue to Channelsea Junction, where they would take the tracks north of the carriage sidings. Immediately beyond Fork Junction, the route passed beneath the main line and ultimately arrived at Stratford Low Level station.   (Railway Magazine)

11. Looking east at Lea Junction around 1922, we see the Lea Curve heading left towards High Meads, and the line to Stratford passing in front of the signal box on the right.   (British Rail)

12. A northwards view of Channelsea Junction in 1922 shows the line from Victoria Park coming in behind the buildings on the left, and the curve to High Meads disappearing behind carriage sidings to the right. (British Rail)

13. This is Fork Junction, looking north from beneath the Liverpool Street - Shenfield main line around the same time. The tracks on the left are those used by Victoria Park services, whilst those on the right ultimately led to Loughton Branch Junction. In between can be seen part of the Stratford Works complex, where the Great Eastern Railway constructed and overhauled its locomotives. (British Rail)

STRATFORD

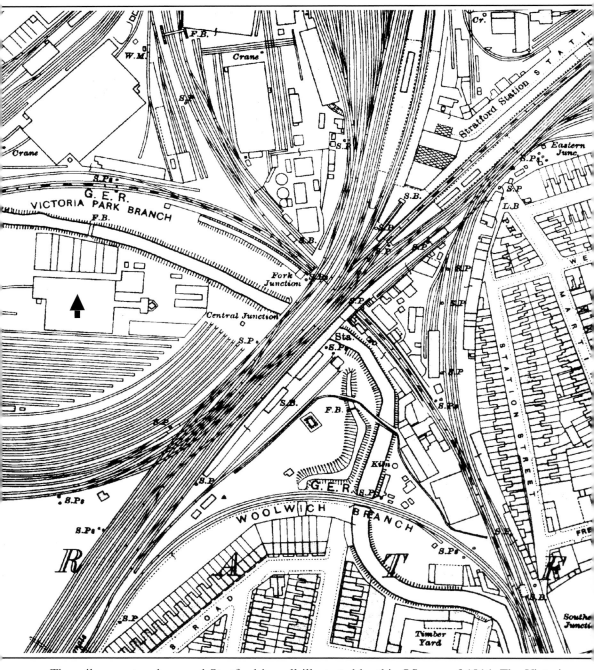

The railway network around Stratford is well illustrated by this OS map of 1914. The Victoria Park branch is shown to the left, lying between the massive GER works complex and the north bank of the Channelsea River. Just to the south-east of Fork Junction, the route can be seen passing beneath the main line before reaching Stratford Low Level. The High Level platforms are described in the Middleton Press Album *Liverpool Street to Ilford*.

14. This southwards view from Fork Junction shows the main line passing above with Stratford Low Level station immediately beyond. This was opened on 16th October 1854, but rebuilt and improved at various times during its history. (British Rail)

15. The Low Level station is seen here in the 1930s, looking north towards Fork Junction. A large board on the down side advises passengers to change should they require destinations on the main line or Ongar branch, whilst behind the lamps on the left, is the distinctive rear wall of High Level Platform No 1. The double storey building to the right of centre provided office accommodation for the District Engineer and his department. (Stations UK)

16. Comparison with the previous photograph shows that by 13th October 1945 when this view was taken, some rebuilding had taken place. The old buildings had been removed, but the large board giving interchange information had been retained and fixed to a new wall. Behind this is a section of the new District Engineers' Office, which was erected in 1938, whilst above, the new High Level platforms are taking shape. These were being reconstructed as part of a 1930s plan, but work was suspended during the Second World War.   (H.C. Casserley)

17. There were two spurs which provided direct connections between the North Woolwich branch and the GE main line. That pointing towards central London was the Stratford Southern Curve, which is seen here in the 1930s, with Class F4 2-4-2T No 7076 hauling a train for Fenchurch Street. The curve opened on 14th June 1847 and was used by passenger services until 28th October 1940. It has since been lifted and its site largely swallowed up by the Stratford terminus of the Jubilee Line. (RAS Marketing)

18. The other connection was the Stratford Eastern Curve, which led from near the country end of the main line station down to a junction just beyond the Low Level platforms. This line, which was never used by regular passenger traffic, opened for freight around 1847 and closed from 12th March 1973. It is seen to the right of this view, which is thought to date from the late 1940s. (Lens of Sutton)

19.   This is the view from the south end of Stratford Low Level on 25th March 1961, as Class N7/5 0-6-2T No 69668 arrives with a train from North Woolwich. The Stratford Eastern Curve diverges to the left, behind the signal.   (A.E. Bennett)

20.   With the advent of the Jubilee Line, the Low Level platforms were completely rebuilt and an impressive new station entrance erected. This is seen on 26th July 2000 soon after an externally restored industrial saddle tank was placed on display outside. The locomotive, named *Robert* was built by the Avonside Engine Company in 1933 and from 1994 had stood on a plinth near Winsor Terrace, Beckton, although it has no actual relevance to the railways of east London. To the left stands the stylish clock tower of Stratford bus station.   (J.E. Connor)

STRATFORD MARKET

The station opened as Stratford Bridge on 14th June 1847 and was located south of the High Street. It was rebuilt in 1860 and the OS map of 1869 shows the layout of the time, with an entrance off Bridge Road.

On 1st October 1879, the Great Eastern Railway opened a vegetable market south of the station, which will be described later.

The station was duly renamed Stratford Market from 1st November 1880 and underwent rebuilding twelve years later to allow space for two additional tracks. These were intended for freight traffic, but before they could be laid, the platforms had to be laterally resited, closer to Bridge Road. This work was completed by 1892, when a new street level building on the south side of High Street replaced the earlier entrance.

21. A view of Stratford Market station in the 1930s, with a train arriving at the down side. The tower on the left gave staff access to the ex-GER printing works which stood in Burford Road to the west of the formation. (Stations UK)

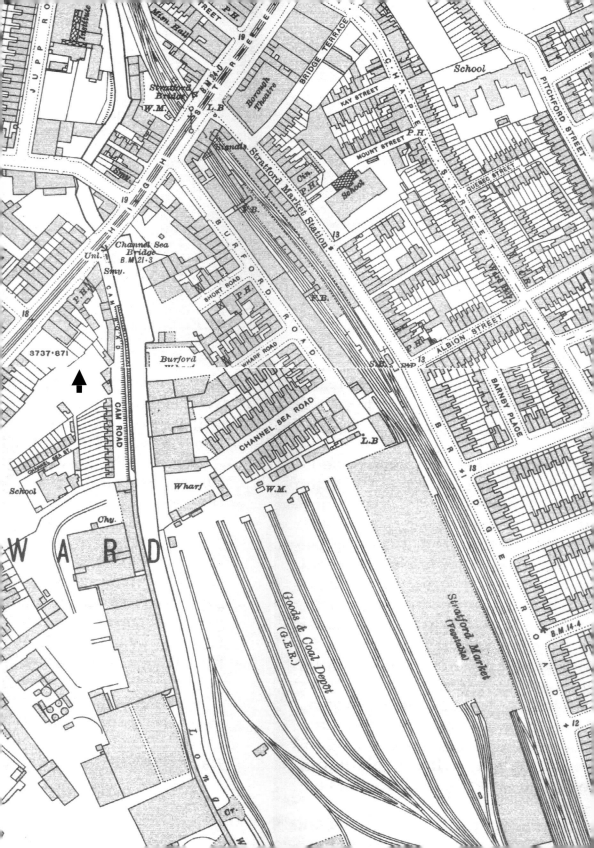

22. The 1892 street level building was a very substantial affair and was linked to the platforms below by means of covered stairways. Because the trains connecting Fenchurch Street or Liverpool Street with the North Woolwich branch took the spur which avoided Stratford Low Level, the station at Stratford Market was once well used. However, patronage dropped off after through services were withdrawn in 1940 and it was closed from 6th May 1957. (Lens of Sutton)

The Ordnance Survey map of 1914 shows the station in its rebuilt form, together with the nearby GER vegetable market and adjoining goods yard. Market trade received a boost following the disastrous fire at Bishopsgate goods depot in 1964, when all perishable traffic from the continent via Harwich was re-routed to Stratford. In 1991 however, new premises opened on the site of the former GER wagon works at Temple Mills and the market facilities at Stratford were closed. The buildings were later demolished to make way for the new Jubilee Line depot, which was completed later in the decade. The goods and coal depot opened around 1880 and had a capacity of 400 wagons, The printing works referred to earlier stood on the east side of Burford Road and was separated from the station by the two goods lines added around 1892. The Eastern Counties Railway established its own printing department in 1844 and this passed to the GER in 1862. Over the years, expansion proved necessary and in 1893 a new four-storey building was constructed, boasting a working area of 46,720 sq.ft. The works was responsible for all the company's printing requirements and remained in use until after nationalisation.

23. In its final weeks the station presented a very sad sight, with its awnings stripped to their bare ironwork. This view looks south on 16th April 1957 and shows the slightly staggered arrangement of the platforms.   (R.M. Casserley)

GREAT EASTERN RAILWAY
Issued subject to Regulations in the Company's Time Tables.
STEPNEY
TO
STRATFORD BRIDGE
Parliamentary Third Class
8996   8996

GREAT EASTERN RAILWAY
Issued subject to Regulations in the Company's Time Tables.
STRATFORD MARKET to
Stratford Mkt   Stratford Mkt
BOW ROAD
BOW RD   BOW RD
1d.   Fare   1d.
THIRD CLASS
9339   9339

GREAT EASTERN RAILWAY.
Issued subject to Regulations in the Company's Time Tables.
STRATFORD MARKET to
Stratford Mkt   Stratford Mkt
CANNING TOWN
Canning Town   Canning Town
1d.   Fare   1d.
924   Third Class
0999   0999

GREAT EASTERN RAILWAY
Issued subject to Regulations in the Company's Time Tables.
STRATFORD MARKET to
Stratford Mkt   Stratford Mkt
HOMERTON
Homerton   Homerton
2d   Fare   2d
THIRD CLASS
9300   9300

10   L. N. E. R.
NOT TRANSFERABLE. This ticket is issued subject to the General Notices, Regulations and Conditions in the Company's current Time Tables, Book of Regulations and Bills. Available for three days, including day of issue
STRATFORD MARKET to
VICTORIA PARK
Fare   S   1½d
THIRD / 1036 \ CLASS
VICTORIA PARK
8265   8265

7 | 8 | 9 | 10 | 11 | 12
BRITISH RAILWAYS   (E)
This ticket is issued subject to the Bye-laws, Regulations and Conditions contained in the Publications & Notices of & applicable to the Railway Executive
PLATFORM TICKET 1d.
Available ONE HOUR on DAY of ISSUE ONLY
NOT VALID IN TRAINS. Not Transferable
STRATFORD MARKET
To be given up when leaving Platform
1 | 2 | 3 | 4 | 5 | 6
6688   6688

24. Four days later, class N7/3 0-6-2T No 69715 was recorded as she stood at the down side with a train for North Woolwich. (A.E. Bennett)

25. The platform awnings were stripped of their covering and valances, and the discarded material moved to the station's southern end to await disposal. This photograph, which was taken on the same date, provides us with a further view of the tower and footways which provided access to the adjoining print works . (A.E. Bennett)

26. Within five years of closure, the platforms and associated structures had been largely demolished, although the street level building remained intact. This was adapted for commercial use in the late 1960s, when a few minor alterations were made, such as windows being added in the rear wall, where stairways once led from the booking hall. Here we see a two-car Cravens diesel multiple unit passing the site of the up platform in 1975. The 1892 goods lines appear on the left.   (J.E. Connor)

27. This view looks north from Bridge Road and dates from the Summer of 1988, three years after the line was electrified. To the left stands the former GER printing works, whilst the distinctive form of Stratford Market's street level building is visible in the distance. By this time the erstwhile freight tracks had been partially lifted and their site behind the old station had been re-used to accommodate berthing facilities. (C. Mansell)

28. Further changes came in the 1990s, with the advent of the Jubilee Line Extension. The short-lived Stratford Market berthing siding was removed and the tracks were temporarily slewed over onto the formation of the old goods lines. Here, a train passes beneath the disused street level building in May 1994, whilst building materials and plant occupy the site of the former platforms. (J.E. Connor)

29. Services between Stratford and North Woolwich were suspended between 29th May 1994 and 29th October 1995 so that the necessary permanent way alterations could be carried out. By 12th February 1995, when this view was taken, the tracks had been replaced on their earlier alignment and the former freight side was being prepared to take the Jubilee Line. At the same time, the old street level building was being renovated and adapted for office use. (L. Collings)

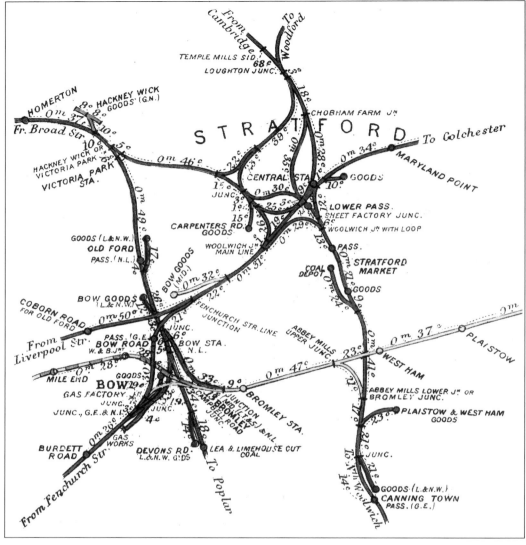

This Railway Clearing House junction diagram of 1915 shows the lines around Stratford, with the North Woolwich branch heading south on the right.

G. E. R.

From _____

TO

STRATFORD MARKET

0 6029

LNER

......................................194...

From OLD LEAKE

POTATOES

TO STRATFORD MARKET

G.E. Section   L.N.E.R. Coy.

Via SPALDING and MARCH

Owner and No. of Wagon	**3**	Sheets in or on Wagon
....		....

No. of Bags..

Whether Carriage ' Paid ' or ' To Pay '.......................

Consignee...

30. This is the main entrance to the former GER market at Stratford as viewed from the south end of Burford Road in the 1980s. The market, which was opened on 1st October 1879 to increase fruit and vegetable traffic on the system, initially comprised eight 60ft x 40ft warehouses. Each of these was provided with a pair of covered sidings, and office accommodation. Produce arrived on early morning trains and was unloaded by the warehouse tenants for immediate sale. In 1907, Stratford Market became a main distribution centre for Elders & Fyffes bananas and within five years, the number of warehouses had grown to twenty-five.

(D. Brennand)

31. Looking north from a footbridge linking Baker's Row with Canning Road in 1988, we see wagons outside Stratford Market and the old printing works in the distance. Although produce was originally delivered to the market by rail, it latterly arrived and was collected by road vehicles. (C. Mansell)

32. The London Underground depot which now occupies the market site measures 190 metres in length by 110 metres in width and features a striking curved parallelogram roof, which is clad in aluminium. The building is a fine piece of modern architecture and has won various awards. Part of its interior is seen here on 20th September 1998, before the Jubilee Line Extension had been brought into public use. (J.E. Connor)

WEST HAM

33. On 14th May 1979 a single island platform was opened at West Ham, to provide inter-change facilities with the London Transport station located on the line above. This view looks north on the opening day and shows work in progress on completing the awning. (J.E. Connor)

34. The island platform of 1979 proved to be fairly short lived, as it had to be rebuilt on a new site, slightly east of the original to accommodate the Jubilee Line. It was last used in May 1994 and its replacement opened on 29th October the following year. Here the adjoining Jubilee Line station is seen whilst nearing completion in March 1998. (G.W. Goslin)

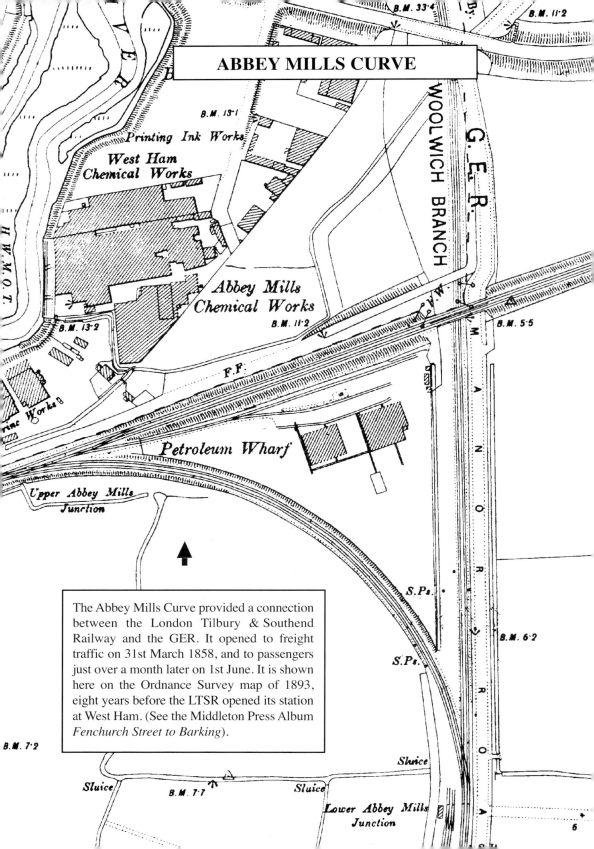

ABBEY MILLS CURVE

Printing Ink Works

West Ham Chemical Works

Abbey Mills Chemical Works

G.E.R. WOOLWICH BRANCH

B.M. 33·4

B.M. 11·2

B.M. 13·1

B.M. 13·2

B.M. 11·2

B.M. 5·5

F.F.

Petroleum Wharf

Upper Abbey Mills Junction

Zinc Works

S.Ps.

B.M. 6·2

S.Ps.

B.M. 7·2

Sluice

Sluice

B.M. 7·7

Sluice

Sluice

Lower Abbey Mills Junction

The Abbey Mills Curve provided a connection between the London Tilbury & Southend Railway and the GER. It opened to freight traffic on 31st March 1858, and to passengers just over a month later on 1st June. It is shown here on the Ordnance Survey map of 1893, eight years before the LTSR opened its station at West Ham. (See the Middleton Press Album *Fenchurch Street to Barking*).

6

35. On 15th June 1957, the Railway Enthusiasts' Club operated its 'Saracen's Head' tour of the London area. This view was taken soon after the train entered the curve from the LTSR line and looks north-west towards Abbey Mills Upper Junction. (A.E. Bennett)

36. The photographer then moved to the opposite side of the train, as it approached the junction with the GER. The Abbey Mills Curve lost its regular passenger service on 27th October 1940 and closed to freight traffic from 27th July 1958. The lower junction was then severed, but the remaining track survived as a siding which was accessed from the LTSR end until 7th August 1960. The present Jubilee and North Woolwich line platforms of West Ham station now adjoin the overbridge seen in the middle distance. (A.E. Bennett)

CANNING TOWN

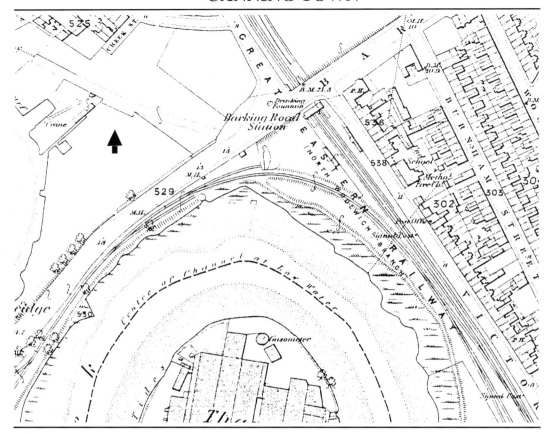

The first station to serve the district was opened on 14th June 1874 and was originally named Barking Road. It stood on the south side of its namesake and is shown on this Ordnance Survey map of 1869, with two platforms accessed by means of a small street level building. Reconstruction took place in 1873 and in July of that year it was renamed Canning Town.

Late in the following decade it was decided to replace the existing premises with a completely new station, and this was opened on the north side of Barking Road, directly opposite its predecessor in 1888. The line seen curving westwards below the station was for goods traffic and led ultimately to the Blackwall Pepper Warehouses.

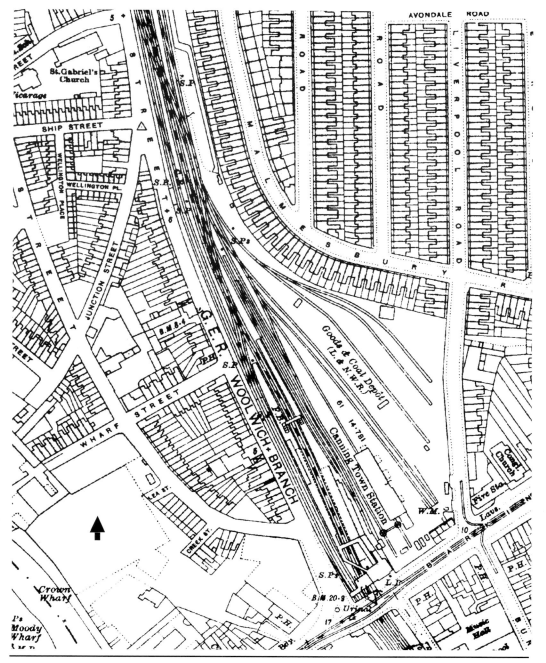

The second station at Canning Town is shown on this Ordnance Survey map of 1914. As built, its only means of public access was through the street level building in Barking Road. However, in 1896, an additional booking office was added on the up side and from then on it seems that the earlier entrance was used for down traffic only. In the previous year, a bay was added on the down side for Victoria Park services and a footbridge was erected at the London end. The goods depot seen immediately east of the passenger station was opened by the London & North Western Railway on 22nd August 1881 and became known as Canning Town North on 1st July 1950.

37. A new street level building facing onto Barking Road was opened in 1932, and the up side booking office was closed. This view shows the later entrance, as it appeared soon after completion, with carved stone panels above the doors showing the station name and company initials. (British Rail)

38. This westward view of the new booking hall interior dates from the same time. The platforms were accessed by means of an arcaded footbridge, which adjoined the gates seen on the right. (British Rail)

39. The 1895 footbridge had disappeared by the mid-1950s, so photographs of it are not very common. Here, the photographer was standing on the down platform in 1942, looking northwards towards the elevated signal cabin which is just visible in the middle distance. White paint has been added at the base of the steps and on lamp posts to make them more visible in the war-time blackout, whilst part of the bay constructed for Victoria Park trains can be seen on the right. (British Rail)

40. Although the street level building was reconstructed in 1932, those serving the platforms remained largely unaltered into the 1950s, although by this time, the down side awning had been reduced in length. This photograph shows Class N7/3 0-6-2T No 69680 standing at the up platform with a train from North Woolwich on 24th August 1957. The canopy valancing seen behind the locomotive was of a type frequently used by the GER, particularly in the London area, during the 1890s and early 1900s. (H.C. Casserley)

41. The platform buildings and attendant awnings were subsequently rationalised. That on the down side remained standing into the second half of the 1960s, but by the start of the following decade had gone, leaving a drastically shortened section of its opposite number, which is shown here. As with Stratford Market, the two goods lines passed behind the passenger station, and were not served by any platform faces. (J.E. Connor)

42. The station saw its final rebuild on this site in the Spring of 1979, when the existing up platform was converted into an island. The down line was slewed over from its earlier alignment, whilst one of the former goods lines was adapted for up passenger traffic. This photograph, looking north from the stairway shows the work in progress. The scrapyard spilling onto the old Victoria Park bay occupied the site of Canning Town North goods depot, which closed on 6th March 1967. (J.E. Connor)

43. As part of the 1979 alterations, the old down platform became redundant and the street level building of 1932 was demolished. The eastern end of this was retained for a very short period and together with a section of the old arcaded footbridge served as public access. Both are seen in this southwards view, but they disappeared soon after it was taken. (J.E. Connor)

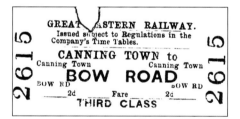

GREAT EASTERN RAILWAY.
Issued subject to Regulations in the
Company's Time Tables.
CANNING TOWN to
Canning Town   Canning Town
BOW ROAD
BOW RD   BOW RD
___2d___   Fare   ___2d___
THIRD CLASS
2615   2615

GREAT EASTERN RAILWAY.
Issued subject to Regulations in the
Company's Time Tables.
No.2] **CANNING TOWN** to
Canning Tn [No.2]   Canning Tn [No.2]
STRATFORD MKT
Stratford Mkt   Stratford Mkt
___1d___   Fare   ___1d___
[90]   Third Class
2444   2444

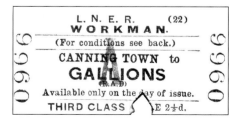

GREAT EASTERN RAILWAY.
Issued subject to Regulations in the
Company's Time Tables.
CANNING TOWN to
Canning Town   Canning Town
TIDAL BASIN
Tidal Basin   Tidal Basin
1d.   Fare   1d.
T RD CLASS
8873   8873

L. N. E. R.
Not transferable. This ticket is issued subject to the
General Notices, Regulations & Conditions in the Co's
current Time Tables. Available on day of issue only
CANNING TOWN to
VICTORIA PARK
Fare   /   S   \   3½d.
THIRD / 1037 \ **CLASS**
VICTORIA PARK
0893   0893

L. N. E. R.   (22)
WORKMAN.
(For conditions see back.)
CANNING TOWN to
GALLIONS
(R.A.D)
Available only on the day of issue.
THIRD CLASS   E 2½d.
0966   0966

PLATFORM.   ADMIT ONE.
CANNING TOWN
THE HOLDER IS PROHIBITED
FROM ENTERING THE
COMPANY'S TRAINS
NOT TRANSFERABLE.
FOR CONDITIONS SEE BACK.
AVAILABLE ON DAY OF ISSUE ONLY
L. N. E. R.   1 A
8963

44. To serve the rebuilt station a completely new street level building was constructed at the corner of Barking Road and Stephenson Street. Here we see its side doorway in 1980, soon after completion. (J.E. Connor)

45. Within a decade, the new building was beginning to look rather the worse for wear. This view was taken from Barking Road in 1993 and shows an entrance to the right which provided access to the island platform when the booking office was closed. (J.L. Crook)

46. This view, looking south from the former down side stairway, shows the station on 3rd April 1988. During rebuilding a small brick shelter was erected on the platform, which also included a staff office. The building became subject to vandalism however and its windows were latterly fitted with metal meshing in an attempt to protect them from being broken. By this time the old LNWR goods depot site had been redeveloped by a well-known DIY merchant. (C. Mansell)

47.   Eventually the shelter was demolished, leaving just the empty windswept island, with no protection from the elements. With the advent of both the Docklands Light Railway and Jubilee Line Extension, it was decided to completely resite the station on the opposite side of the main road, so the existing premises saw no further improvements. This photograph shows the station in its final days, with vegetation from the old down platform encroaching onto the track. (J.L. Crook)

48. Canning Town station closed when the service between Stratford Low Level and North Woolwich was suspended from 29th May 1994 to allow realignment. The track was soon lifted and by 10th June 1994 when this view was taken, demolition of the raft which once supported the street level building was well under way. (J.E. Connor)

49. The replacement station was positioned slightly south of the original 1847 site. Here we see the new island platform under construction on 14th April 1995, with the alignment of the Jubilee Line Extension to the right. (L. Collings)

50. The new station opened with the resumption of North Woolwich branch services on 29th October 1995 and is seen here two days later with a train for Willesden Junction arriving. The Docklands Light Railway opened its adjoining station on 5th March 1998 and the Jubilee Line, under construction on the right, followed on 14th May 1999. (J.E. Connor)

BLACKWALL GOODS DEPOT

Blackwall goods depot was located on the west side of Bow Creek and opened in June 1848. The short branch was authorised during 1846 and was intended to bring rail access to some existing pepper warehouses and a wharf belonging to the East India Dock Company. Upon opening, the warehouses were leased in perpetuity to the Eastern Counties Railway and eventually sold to the GER in the 1880s.

The depot, often referred to as 'The Blackwall Pepper Warehouses', was reached by means of a line which branched off to the south of Canning Town and headed initially towards Stratford. By means of a 180ft radius curve and a gradient of 1 in 30, it then swung towards Bow Creek, which it crossed on a single-track bridge. The tight nature of these approaches resulted in heavy restrictions being placed on the motive power used, and for its entire existence, only short,

four-coupled engines could be employed.

Within the depot itself, wagons were initially manoeuvred by horses, but these were later replaced by eleven electric capstans. A pair of electrically operated cranes were installed in 1961, but by this time, road competition had taken away much of the former traffic and closure came on 6th March 1967.

Near the junction with the North Woolwich line stood Canning Town goods depot. This dated back to the route's earliest days, but later underwent various changes. It was renamed Canning Town South on 1st July 1950 and survived to have its old steam cranes replaced by electric in the early 1960s. By then its days were numbered however and it closed on 1st July 1968.

The overgrown tracks remained for a while, but were eventually lifted and the site was partially utilised for the new Canning Town station complex.

51. This is the entrance to the Blackwall goods depot, as viewed from the opposite side of East India Dock Road in the late 1950s. After closure, much of the site was used as a scrapyard and some of the track remained in position. With the general redevelopment of the area however, all was swept away and the depot, like the delightful Austin car seen on the left, passed into history. (Norfolk Railway Society)

The branch serving Blackwall goods depot is shown to the left of this Ordnance Survey map of 1914, which has been reduced in size to include its junction with the passenger line on the right.

THAMES WHARF JUNCTION

Thames Wharf Junction, located between Canning Town and Tidal Basin stations was where the original North Woolwich line of 1847 diverged from the 1855 deviation, which was made necessary by construction of the Victoria Dock. The entrance to this cut through the alignment of the branch and although a swing bridge was provided, its frequent operation would have delayed train services, therefore the new line was built at the dock company's expense.

The Ordnance Survey map of 1914 shows both routes, with the earlier formation immediately to the west of Dock Road. The tracks to the extreme left are part of the once extensive internal dock system, which from 1909 was managed by the Port of London Authority.

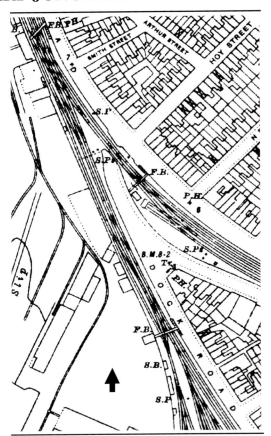

52. On 25th March 1961, Class N7/3 0-6-2T No 69707 was recorded soon after negotiating Thames Wharf Junction with a train for North Woolwich. The earlier route, which was retained for freight, can be seen in the foreground.   (A.E. Bennett)

53. From 1855, the original route became known officially as Woolwich Abandoned Line, although it was more generally referred to as The Silvertown Tramway. This view, taken on 15th August 1962, looks south from Thames Wharf Yard and shows its commencement. The cobbled road surface and swan-necked street lamps help to complete an evocative picture of a lost East End. (A.E. Bennett)

TIDAL BASIN

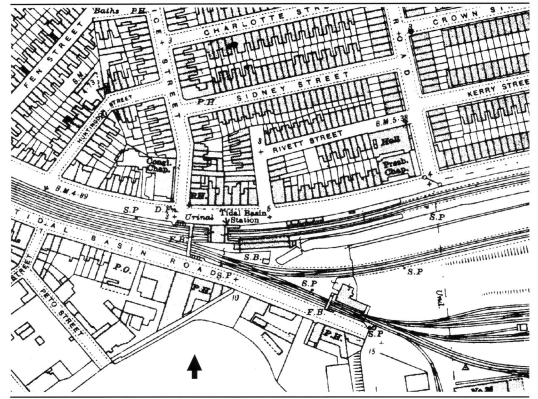

Tidal Basin station was opened in 1858, but underwent various changes throughout its existence, with its most significant rebuild being authorised in 1883. As can be seen from this Ordnance Survey map of 1914, lack of space resulted in the booking office being above the tracks and having to be accessed by stairways from the adjoining street. South of the passenger line lies part of the railway network which once served the Port of London.

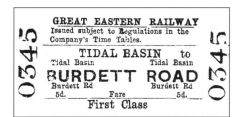

54. The station was badly damaged in an air raid on 29th March 1941, when the London Blitz was at its height. This view, looking west along Victoria Dock Road gives an idea of the scale of destruction which thousands of Londoners had to contend with on an almost nightly basis. The stairs which provided public access to the station are visible to the right of the building. (British Rail)

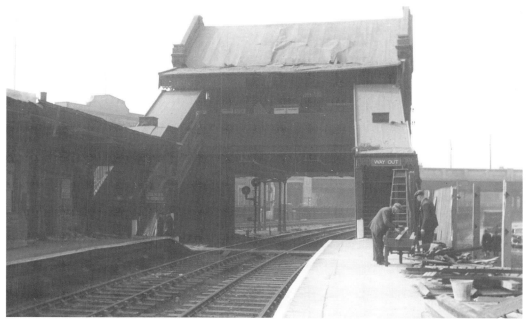

55. The station was tidied up and remained open, but with the local populace depleted by conscription and evacuation, there was little demand, so it was permanently closed from 15th August 1943. Judging by the state of the main building roof in both these views, it had no doubt received attention from the Luftwaffe at an earlier date.   (British Rail)

Liverpool Street (dep	...	...	...	...	7 22		mov	2	...	4 25		...	...	1082		...		1128			
Bishopsgate	...	...	...	...	7 24		...	3 24	...	3 28		...	...	1034		...		1120			
Bethnal Green Junc	...		c	...	7 27		...	3 29		d	9 33		d	...	1037		...	d	1133			
Coborn Rd. for Old Frd	...			...	7 32		...	3 34			9 37			...	1041		...		1138			
Fenchurch Street d	...	6 15	7 11	...	7 52	3 20	...	9 0	9 15		9 40	9 58	1020		1040		11 0		1120		114	
Stepney	...	6 23	7 23	...	7 55	3 24	...	9 5	9 24		9 48	10 3	1026		1046		11 5		1126		114	
Burdett Road	...	6 25	7 25	...	8 0	3 28	...	9 7	9 26	nov	9 48	10 5	1028		1048		11 7		1128		114	
Bow Road	...	6 28		...	8 3	3 31	...	9 10				10 8					1110				114	
Stratford Market	5 17	5 25	6 30	6 34		7 82	8 38	8 41	9 15	b	9 42	a	1013	a	1047	1058		a	1144	a		a
Canning Town *	5 22	5 30	6 35	6 39	7 34	7 42	3 12	3 43	8 47	9 19	9 35	9 46	9 56	1017	1036	1052	1056	11 3	1119	1136	1149	1156
Vict. Tidal Basin	5 26	5 34	6 38	6 42	7 37	7 45	3 16	3 46	3 50	9 22	3 3	9 51	9 59	1020	1039	1055	1059	11 6	1122	1139	1152	1159
Docks (Custom House	5 32	5 41	6 44	6 45	7 40	7 48	3 19	3 49	3 53	9 25	9 41	9 54	10 2	1023	1042	1058	11 2	11 9	1125	1142	1155	12 2
Gallions † arr	...	...	6 51	7	7 55	3	9 35	9	5 9	22	9 38	9 51	...	1011	1011	10 7	...	1052	1111	1111	...	1137	1152	1211	1211
Beckton arr	...	5 49	...	...	...	...	...	...	...	8 9	...	...	...	...	1017	1117	1117		1137	1152	1211	1211
Silvertown	5 36		6 49	7 4	7 52	3 23	3 53	3 57		9 24		9 58	10 6	1027		11 2	11 6		1129		1159	12 6
North Woolwich	5 40		6 53	7 48	7 57	3 27	3 57	9 1	9 33		9	10 2	1010	1031		11 6	1110		1133		12 3	1211
Woolwich Town arr	...	...	7 12	3	5 8	8	3 35	8	9 0	9 45			1010	1022	1046		1125	1125		1140		1220	122

Liverpool St d	...	1229		...	1 28		...	...	3 20		...	...	4 25	
Bishopsgate	...	1230		...	1 30		...	...	3 22		...	...	4 30	
Bethnal Grn J	d	1233		d	1 33		d	d	3 25	d	...	d	4 33	
Coborn Road		1238			1 38				3 30		...		4 37	
Fnchrch St.	12 0	1220		1240	1 0	1 20		1 40	1 0		2 40		3 20		9 40	4 0	4 20		4 40	4
Stepney	12 5	1226		1245	1 5	1 26		1 46	1 5		2 26	2 26		2 46		3		28		3 46	4 4	4
Burdett Rd.	12 7	1228		1248	1 7	1 28		1 48	1 7		2 28	2 24		2 48		1	3 7	1 28		4 44	4
Bow Road	1210				1 10							3 16			4 10	
Stratford Mkt	1218	a	1244	a	1 15	a	1 44	a	1 18	2 20	a	2 36	1 48	a	2 58	3 15	a	3 36	a	42	a
Canning Tn.*	1219	1236	1249	1256	1 19	1 40	1 56	2 18	1 30	2 26	2 40	1 52	2 58	3 3	3 19	3 6	3 41	3 56	4	36	4 49	4 56	19
Vict.|Tdl. Bsn	1222	1239	1252	1259	1 22	1 39	1 52	1 50	10 22	2 33	2 89	2 43	2 54	2 59	3 6	3 23	3 59	3 44	3 59	4	31	4 52	4 59	22
Dcks|CHouse	1225	1249	1255	1 2	1 25	1 42	1 55	2	1 25	2 36	2 42	2 47	6	57	2 3	9 3	76	4 2	3 47	1	4 42	4 57	5	25
Gallions †a	1237	1252	1 10	1 11	1 37	1 52	2 10	2 11	2 37	...	2 52	1 56	3 11	5 11	...	3 87	3 52	4 11	1 11	4	4 52	5	25	5 40
Beckton ar	...	...	...	...	...	...	...	1 4	...	2 52	...	3 17	...
Silvertown	1229		1259	6	1 29		1 59	2	2 29		1 3		3 2		3 6	4	4 25		4 595	5	25
Nth Woolwch	1233		1	31	101	33		1 2	32	101	32			5	10		3 38		3 55	4 10	4		5 10	5 33
WoolwchTn	1240		1	201	40		2	102	201	40			3	40		4	54	22	4 4		5	185	185	5 40

Liverpool St d	...	...	5 42		8 38		7 36	8 9	9 35 8	...	103.		1184	
Bishopsgate	...	...	5 44		6 40		7 38	8 81	9 37 8	...	104		1186	
BethnalGrnJ	...	...	5 47		6 43		7 41	8 84	9 40	...	104		1189	
Coborn Road	...	...	5 52		6 48		7 46	8 39	9 44	...	104		1144	
Fnchrch St.	5 27		5 51	6 27	6 57	7 27	...	7 57	9 0	...	9	1 57	1057	
Stepney	5 33		5 57	6 33	...	7 37	8	8	9 5	...	10 3	1 1		
Burdett Rd	5 35		5 59	6 35	...	7 35	8	8	9 5	...	10 5	1 1		
Bow Road	5 58		6 2	6 38	...	7 87	38	8	9 11	...	10 8	1 1		
Stratfrd Mkt.	5 20	5 44	5 59 6	8 6	44	6 44	7 44	7 52	8 14	8 45	9 17	9 509	55	1014	105	1114	1170		
Canning Tn.*	5 24	5 49	6	4 6	136	49	6 59	7 19	7 49	7	578	19	8	50	9	22 9	549 0	1019	1059	1119	1180	
Vict.|Tdl. Bsn	5 28	5 52	6	7 6	16	6	52 7	2	7 22	7	528	0 8	22 8	53 9	23 9	57 10	3	1022	11	7	1122	1159	
Dcks CHouse	5 35	5 55	6	10 7	19	6	55 7	5	7 25 7	55 8	3 9	26 10	0 10	6	1025	11	7	125	12 2	
Gallions †a	...	...	6 29	6 29	...		...	...			...	...		
Beckton ar	5 43		...	...	...	...	...	...	1015	...		
Silvertown	...	...	5 69	6	14 6	23	6	69 7	9 7	29 7	59 8	7	8	29 9	0 9	32 10	4	1029	11	1125	12 6	
Nth Woolwch	...	4	81	18 6	27 7	8 7	18 7	8 8 7	83 8	38	118	38 9	4 9	36 10	8	1033	1115	1138	1210	
WoolwchTn	...	6	106	35 6	40 7	12 7	20 7	40 8	17 8	17 8	40 9	18 9	40 10	18 9	4	1017	...	1218	114	1218	

a Run via Bromley.   b Call at Bromley.   c Calls at Leman Street and Shadwell.   d Through to Royal Albert Docks.

SUNDAYS.—Liverpool St. to Woolwich at 9 18 and 10 38 mrn.; 1 37, 2 41, 3 36, 4 35, 5 36, 4 36, 7 34, 9 85, 9 37, and 10 33 aft. Fenchurch St. to Woolwich at 8 20, 9 50, and 10 57 mrn.; 12 57, 1 52, 2 57, 3 57, 4 57, 5 52, 7 27,7 57, 8 57, and 9 57 aft. Stratford Market to Beckton at 5 25 mrn. and 9 57 aft. To Woolwich at 8 6 mrn. * Station for Barking Road.   † Royal Albert Dock.

NORTH and SOUTH WOOLWICH FERRY.—Extra Ferry Trips.—From North Woolwich at 5 20, 5 40, 6, 6 20, 6 38, 6 52, 7, 7 32, and 9 18 mrn. Sundays at 12 33 aft.

1882

G. E. R.
—
Tidal Basin

G. E. R.
—
From _____
TO
TIDAL BASIN

56. This photograph, snatched from a passing enthusiasts' special, gives us an extremely rare post-war view of Tidal Basin station. The down platform and the stairway serving it appear to have been in reasonably good order, although the attendant buildings were destroyed in 1941. Those on the opposite side are known to have survived a little longer however, although whether they lasted until 14th April 1951, when this picture, was taken is unknown. (E.A. Course)

57. By the early 1950s the main building was in a very derelict condition, and being located above the tracks it was no doubt removed fairly promptly in the interests of safety. At the same time it seems likely that the platforms disappeared as well, as by later in the decade, all that remained was a low section of wall on the down side and gaps beside the line. For this view, the photographer was standing on the steps of a public footbridge, looking south along Victoria Dock Road, as an N7 hauled train approached from North Woolwich. Part of the land to the right was later utilised to accommodate the Dockland Light Railway Beckton route and the DLR Royal Victoria station is located nearby. (Stephenson Locomotive Society)

CUSTOM HOUSE

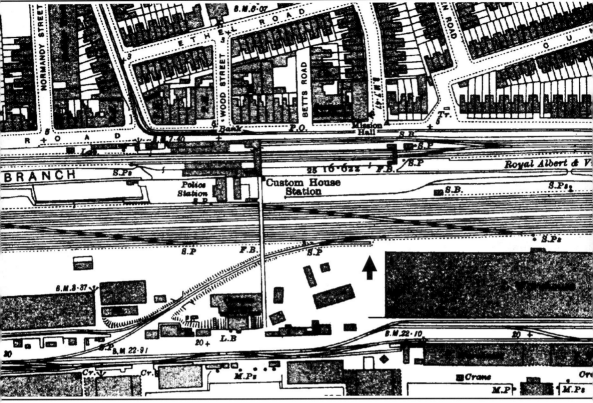

Custom House station opened in the closing months of 1855, but the premises shown on this 1914 Ordnance Survey map date from a rebuilding of 1891. By then, the area north of the line was largely taken up by housing, but immediately to the south lay the dock estate, with its internal railway system and exchange sidings. The station was sometimes referred to as 'Custom House, Victoria Dock', but the suffix was scarcely if ever, shown on tickets and in later days at least, was not included on the nameboards.

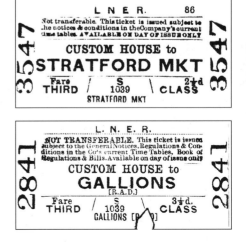

58. Looking west from the station footbridge on 1st September 1934, we see Class F4 2-4-2T No 7189 arriving with a train for North Woolwich. (H.C. Casserley)

59. The area around the docks was devastated by the first major raid of the London Blitz on 7th September 1940, which became known locally as 'Black Saturday'. This view shows the east end of Custom House station three days later, after clearing up operations had started. To the left, some open wagons and a rake of coaches stand at the bay platform intended for Gallions trains. The coaches may well have been those used on this service, but the Gallions branch closed after the bombing and never reopened. (British Rail)

60. The station was subsequently repaired, but the up side building continued to show evidence of its wartime damage and never received a replacement awning. This photograph looks west and shows Class N7/3 0-6-2T No 69714 arriving with a North Woolwich train on 15th April 1961. The footbridge continued beyond the up platform and led, by way of a manned gateway, into the adjoining dock estate. (A.E. Bennett)

61. The former Gallions branch bay retained its track well into the 1960s and was used as a siding. It is seen to the right of this view taken in the previous decade, which shows another member of the N7 class arriving from Stratford. The prominent station nameplate was of LNER origin and the shape of its backing board indicates that the lozenge shaped company logo was previously displayed at its top. (Stephenson Locomotive Society)

62. During the 1950s and early 1960s, the N7s were a familiar sight on the North Woolwich branch. Here No 69645 is seen arriving at Custom House with a down train. (B.P. Pask)

63. The down side building of 1891 survived until 1969, when it was demolished and replaced by a rather spartan shelter. This view looks east and includes the distinctive 'Flying Angel' seamen's mission in the background to the right. This was opened in 1933 and in recent years has been used as a hostel. From 28th March 1994, the much rebuilt Custom House became an interchange station, when the Docklands Light Railway branch from Poplar to Beckton was brought into public use. (I. Baker)

64. Looking from the station's eastern end in the 1950s, we see the bay platform to the left and the main passenger line on the right. At this time everything was still fully signalled, with semaphore arms referring to the Beckton and Albert Dock branches, as well as the route serving North Woolwich. In the distance, on the north side of Victoria Dock Road, stands a row of 'prefabs', which provided much-needed housing in war-torn parts of London during the 1940s, 50s and 60s. Despite their temporary nature, a few were still standing in 2000, but those in this photograph disappeared many years ago. The signal box survived until 1985, when it was destroyed by fire. (Stephenson Locomotive Society)

65. We return to the footbridge, but this time look east on 15th April 1961 as Class N7 No 69714 approaches with an up train. Behind the tall concrete fence on the right lie some of the PLA exchange sidings, which were established in the 1870s and joined the GER at Thames Wharf Junction. At one time the yard comprised thirty-five sidings, and were all laid in a manner to allow gravity shunting. (A.E. Bennett)

66. The Port of London Authority once had an extensive stud of steam locomotives, and a number of these were allocated to a shed within the dock estate at Custom House. Here, Austerity type 0-6-0ST No 82 was recorded passing the shed in September 1957 with four PLA insulated vans. These were generally used for transporting bananas from in-coming ships to the exchange sidings, where they would be off-loaded and transferred to BR vehicles. (R.C. Riley)

67. The depot at Custom House provided those fortunate enough to gain admittance, with the opportunity to look at some of the PLA locomotives at close quarters. This is 0-6-0T No 70 which was built by Hawthorn Leslie in 1922 and remained in traffic until 1955. (J.E. Connor Collection)

68. PLA 0-6-0T No 73 was a product of Hudswell Clarke and dated from 1927. This view shows her working in the sidings near Custom House on 8th February 1959, the year of her withdrawal. To the far right we catch a glimpse of 'Victoria Dock D', one of four signal boxes which once controlled the local internal system. (A.R. Goult)

69. Diesel traction had completely replaced steam within the Port of London by 1963 and the locomotives were subsequently scrapped. Here we see a forlorn line-up near Custom House shed, with one of the new diesel shunters just visible to the right. The steam loco nearest the camera is Hudswell Clark 0-6-0T No 76, which was built in 1943 and acquired by the PLA three years later. Next to her stands 'Austerity' 0-6-0ST No 82, which was supplied by Robert Stephenson & Hawthorns and also dated from 1943. The internal system serving the Royal Docks closed in 1970. (Stephenson Locomotive Society)

EAST OF CUSTOM HOUSE

When a connecting channel was built to link the existing Victoria Dock and the new Royal Albert Dock in the late 1870s, the line between Custom House and Silvertown had to be provided with a swingbridge adjoining the west side of Connaught Road. Once again, it was felt that the constant coming and going of ships would result in disruption to train services, so a deviation had to be constructed, to take the tracks beneath the channel in a 600yd tunnel. This was opened in 1876 and the earlier route was taken over by the dock company. Understandably, it became known to staff as the 'High Level Line', although its official title was 'The Transferred Portion'.

70. Looking north on 25th March 1961 we see the swingbridge, which had a length of 183ft and a span of 90ft. Not only did it carry the double track line, but it also accommodated a 40ft wide section of Connaught Road itself. There was once a signal box at either end, but that on the north side of the channel was removed around 1935, leaving the other which is shown here. (A.E. Bennett)

7 | 8 | 9 | 10 | 11 | 12 **British Transport Commission (E)** **CUSTOM HOUSE** **PLATFORM TICKET 1D.** Available One Hour on Day of Issue only Not Valid in Trains Not Transferable To be given up when leaving Platform FOR CONDITIONS SEE OVER 1 | 2 | 3 | 4 | 5 | 6	7 | 8 | 9 | 10 | 11 | 12 **British Railways Board (E)** **CUSTOM HOUSE** **PLATFORM TICKET 2d.** Available one hour on day of issue only. Not valid in trains. Not transferable. To be given up when leaving platform. For conditions see over 1 | 2 | 3 | 4 | 5 | 6

71. The deviation followed the 1855 route very closely and surfaced a short distance to the north-west of Silvertown station. This photograph, taken on 25th March 1961, looks down from near Connaught Road and shows the earlier line to the left and the southern tunnel portal of its replacement on the right. The Connaught Road swing bridge and its attendant signal box is just visible in the distance. (A.E. Bennett)

72. This is the junction at the Silvertown end on the same day, with Class N7/5 0-6-2T No 69668 about to descend into the tunnel with an up train. From both directions, the tunnel was approached by a 1 in 50 gradient and because of this, the number of wagons on goods trains had to be restricted. Occasionally, if the load was too great, or the tunnel happened to be blocked in some way, freight workings had to be routed over the high level route instead. (A.E. Bennett)

SILVERTOWN

73. Silvertown station was opened on 19th June 1863. The area took its name from a small colony of houses which accommodated the workforce of S.W. Silver, who constructed a nearby factory in 1852 for the manufacture of various rubber products including ebonite and cable. This view, looking south-east from North Woolwich Road, is thought to date from the 1880s. (D. Brennand Collection)

74. The station was rebuilt around 1885, when it received a new booking hall, extended awning and covered footbridge. Here we look down from a public footbridge at the west end of the platforms and see how busy the premises could be in the 1930s, when the North Woolwich branch provided a vital link for workers travelling to and from the local factories and docks. (Stations UK)

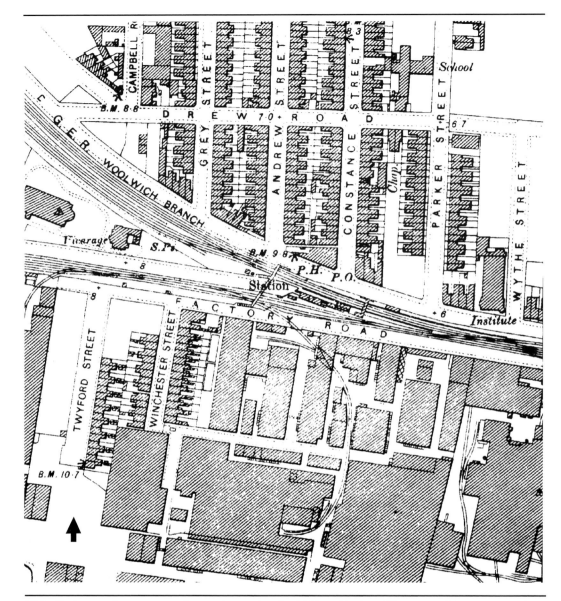

This Ordnance Survey map shows the station in 1893, with the Silvertown Tramway running immediately north of Factory Road, and the later route from Custom House coming in above.

75. The station entrance was located on the up side and took the shape of a doorway beneath the signal box, which led into the gas-lit booking hall. This view dates from the 1950s or 60s, by which time, the footbridge, just visible in the middle distance, had lost its roofing. (Lens of Sutton)

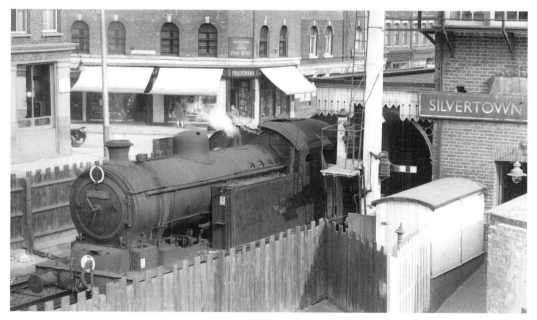

76. Looking down from the north side of the public footbridge on 25th March 1961, we see Class N7/5 0-6-2T No 69668 with a train from North Woolwich. Behind her, on the far corner of Constance Street stands Silvertown Station Post Office. (A.E. Bennett)

77. The public footbridge at the west end of the station was a good vantage point for photographing trains. Here, Class N7/5 0-6-2T No 69668 has just arrived with an up service on 25th March 1961. (A.E. Bennett)

78. Also on 25th March 1961, the same locomotive is seen at the opposite end of the station with a down train. The Silvertown Tramway runs behind the up platform, whilst just visible in the distance is the tower of St. Mark's Church, designed by the architect S.S. Teulon and erected in 1861-2. (A.E. Bennett)

79. At the west end of the down platform was an additional exit, which comprised a short flight of steps leading onto North Woolwich Road and a small hut for the ticket collector. This was also used for the purchase of tickets when the main booking office was closed, and the short section of awning was presumably to offer shelter to those waiting in the queue. (R.K. Blencowe Collection)

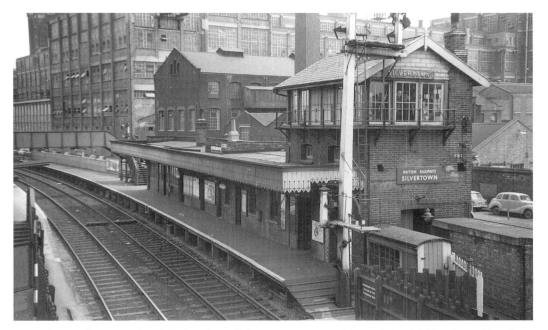

80. The station remained little altered for many years although by 1963 when this view was taken, the LNER nameboard over the main entrance had been replaced by one of the standard British Railways type in vitreous enamel with white lettering on a dark blue background. (J.S. Phillips)

81. The signal box was later closed and removed, but no other major changes took place for some time. Here we look west in the mid-1970s and see that even at this late stage, the platforms were still gaslit. Since 25th August 1969, all passenger traffic east of Custom House had been routed onto the former down line, although the up track was retained for surviving freight traffic. (I. Baker)

82. The station was rebuilt in the late 1970s, with a platform on the former down side only. This view, looking west, was taken on 3rd April 1988 and shows one of the Southern Region Class 416/3 EPB units which were introduced to the route with electrification on 13th May 1985. The construction of an airport on erstwhile dock land nearby resulted in Silvertown receiving the suffix "& London City Airport" from 4th October 1987. (C. Mansell)

NORTH WOOLWICH

83. The station was bombed during the 'Black Saturday' air-raid of 7th September 1940, when its awnings were largely destroyed and a train standing at the platform was badly damaged. The main building escaped fairly lightly, although when subsequently patched-up, its original roofline was not restored. (British Rail)

84. A public footbridge a little to the north west of the station provided a good vantage point for photographing train movements. Here, Class N7/4 0-6-2T No 69602 is seen departing with a train for Palace Gates on 8th September 1956. The goods yard, visible to the right, was rationalised in the 1960s and closed from 7th December 1970. (A.E. Bennett)

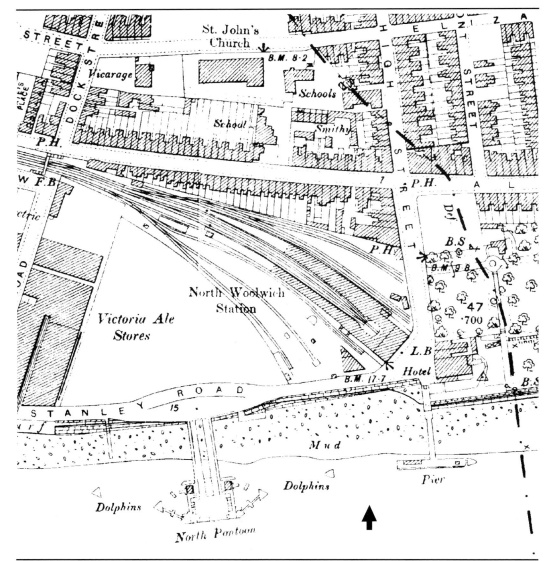

Here we see North Woolwich terminus, as it appeared on the Ordnance Survey map of 1894. At this time it boasted three platform roads, two of which ended in a small locomotive turntable. The goods yard, located to the south-west of the site was subsequently enlarged and by the early 1960s comprised eleven sidings. Immediately opposite the station entrance was the GER pier, where passengers were charged a penny to travel by ferry to Woolwich proper on the south side of the Thames. This service fell into decline after the newly-formed London County Council began competing with a free ferry from March 1889, although it managed to cling-on until 1st October 1908. The LCC boats operated from a separate pier, a little up-stream from the GER and this can be seen slightly left of centre with the legend 'North Pontoon'. The open land shown to the right of North Woolwich station started life as 'The Royal Pavilion Gardens', when opened by the Eastern Counties Railway in 1851 to attract extra custom to the line. They once included a dance hall and other attractions, but rowdiness amongst visitors led to their closure and conversion into a public park in 1890.

85. Following the loss of their awnings in 1940, the platforms at North Woolwich appeared very bare and spartan. In this view, we are looking from behind the buffer-stops, as a two-car Metro-Cammell diesel multiple unit awaits departure for Stratford. The gap between the tracks had previously accommodated a run-round road which was rendered redundant following the end of locomotive operation on the line. (J.E. Connor)

86. When opened on 14th June 1847, North Woolwich terminus was originally provided with wooden buildings. These were removed in 1854 however and replaced by the fine edifice seen here. The view dates from the late 1970s, by which time the premises were showing distinct signs of neglect. (J.L. Crook)

87. After the section east of Custom House became effectively two-single lines from 25th August 1969, there was no longer a need for more than one track at North Woolwich station. Therefore the other was subsequently lifted and the platform left to become derelict. By the mid-1970s, the main building had been boarded-up and the erstwhile goods yard site was being used for parking road vehicles. (I. Baker)

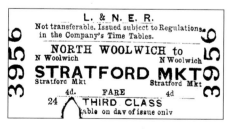

88. In 1979 a new entrance was constructed on the south-western side of the station and the earlier building closed. The platform situation then reversed, with the track being re-laid on the up side whilst the other fell into disuse. (J.E. Connor)

89. Fortunately the main building of 1854 was later acquired by the Passmore Edwards Trust and converted into 'The Old Station Museum'. This also incorporated the down side platform and the former turntable area, where ex-GER 0-4-0ST No 229 was placed on display. This view was taken in November 1984, a few days before the museum was officially opened by HM Queen Elizabeth, The Queen Mother. It was open during Summer weekends in 2000. (J.E. Connor)

NORTH WOOLWICH PIER

90. Although the GER ferry service to what the company referred to as 'South Woolwich' ceased in 1908, the pier on the north side was retained for the use of pleasure steamers and passed into LNER ownership at the Railway Grouping of 1923. Here we see the entrance in 1947. (British Rail)

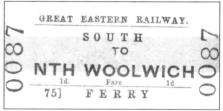

GREAT EASTERN RAILWAY.
SOUTH
TO
NTH WOOLWICH
1d.   Fare   1d
75]   FERRY
0087   0087

91. This view, taken at the same date, shows the close proximity between the entrance and the station. Passengers passed through the gate leading from the point where High Street joined Stanley Road, then made their way across the pier towards the landing stage. (British Rail)

92. At the south end of the pier, passengers reached the landing stage, where, perhaps not surprisingly, the wooden buildings resembled those often seen on railway stations. This view, looking east, was taken in November 1947 and shows the office, where GER tickets were presumably issued for cross-river journeys. The office on the other side offered through bookings to destinations on other parts of the company's system. (British Rail)

93. We are now looking west and see the LCC free ferry waiting at its pier slightly up-stream. The railway-owned building furthest from the camera provided waiting accommodation, whilst that next to it was the office seen above. The one in the right foreground was a customs block, although why this should have been provided seems a bit puzzling, as even in later days the only regular traffic was to destinations such as Southend and Margate. (British Rail)

2. Beckton Branch

94. After diverging from the North Woolwich line to the east of Custom House, the Beckton branch passed over Connaught Road by means of a level crossing, then reached a small goods and coal depot known as West Ham South. This was sited to the north of the line and functioned from around 1892 until 7th December 1964. Here we have a view of its office, as seen from a passing enthusiasts railtour on 29th April 1961. (A.E. Bennett)

95. The second, and final level crossing on the branch was at East Ham Manor Way. On 22nd June 1901, East Ham Corporation introduced a service of electric trams to New Beckton, which crossed the line here, and a cabin known as Beckton Tramway Crossing Box was installed to control both trains and trams with semaphore signals. That shown here however, is almost certainly a post-nationalisation replacement, as its appearance is more reminiscent of boxes erected by the Midland Railway than those of the GER. The photo looks east and was taken on a foggy afternoon in 1967, after the box had closed. A view of the earlier box appears in the Middleton Press album *East Ham and West Ham Tramways*. (J.E. Connor)

BECKTON

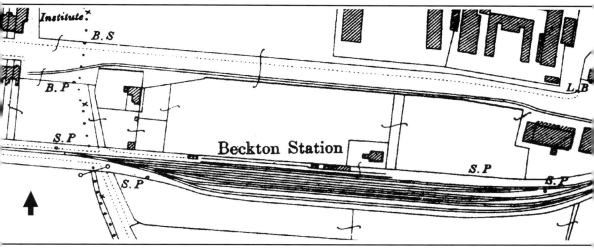

The passenger station at Beckton, shown on this Ordnance Survey map of 1894, comprised a single gaslit platform, which was positioned on the north side of the line. It was located 2miles 1chain from Custom House and was accessed by means of a footpath which led from the east end of Winsor Terrace, named after one of the gas company directors, Frederick Albert Winsor. Winsor Terrace is shown, un-named, near the top of the map, with some of the houses erected for gasworks employees just visible to the left.

The station had a signal box, waiting shelter and booking office, although the latter was rarely manned in its final years. In fact, apart from the signalman, Beckton station was often un-staffed and tickets from in-coming passengers had to be collected at Custom House.

Beyond the platform, the tracks continued into the vast internal system which served the gas works and its adjoining by-products factory. There were also sidings beside the station, which were used for marshalling out-going goods trains. Loaded coke wagons, often around forty at a time, would be pushed into these by one of the little gas works engines, then a main line locomotive would couple on and take them to their eventual destination.

G. E. R.

Beckton

96. Views of Beckton station whilst still open to passenger traffic are few and far between. Here we are looking east, with the platform on our left and the exchange sidings to the right. It is not known when the photograph was taken, but it seems likely to date from the 1930s. (J.E. Connor Collection)

97. Passenger traffic, which had declined through tram and bus competition, was disrupted by the onset of the Blitz and permanently withdrawn in December 1940. This view shows the waiting shelter after closure, with the former ticket office to the right. Goods traffic declined drastically in the 1960s and official closure came in February 1971. By early 1973 the branch track had been lifted. (J.E. Connor Collection)

BECKTON GASWORKS SYSTEM

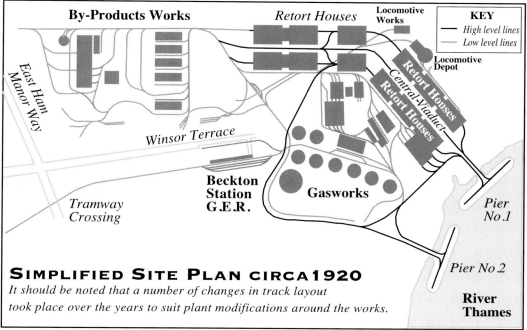

By-Products Works   *Retort Houses*   Locomotive Works

KEY
— High level lines
— Low level lines

Locomotive Works

Locomotive Depot

Retort Houses
Central Viaduct
Retort Houses

East Ham Manor Way

Winsor Terrace

Beckton Station G.E.R.

Tramway Crossing

Gasworks

Pier No.1

Pier No.2

SIMPLIFIED SITE PLAN CIRCA 1920
It should be noted that a number of changes in track layout took place over the years to suit plant modifications around the works.

River Thames

(London Railway Record October 1994)

Before our brief tour of the Beckton works, which first produced gas on 25th November 1870, it is perhaps best to look at this map. The Gas Light & Coke Company's internal railway system was essential for the operation of the works. When fully developed, the 269 acre site was crammed with 41 miles of standard gauge track, all of which was fully signalled. Of this, 32 miles were at ground level whilst the other 9 were carried on steel viaduct.

The track comprised largely of 56lb flat-bottom rail, and check rails were provided on some of the sharp curves. Obviously on a system such as this there were numerous curves, and the sharpest of these had a radius of 50ft.

Signal boxes and ground frames were installed where necessary, and by the early years of the twentieth century, there were no fewer than fourteen of these around the site. There was a set of engine whistle codes in force to enable signalmen to recognise which route a particular train was due to take.

The railway was so vast that around fifty engines were required for its operation. It even had its own fully equipped locomotive works, which in addition to the maintenance of existing motive power, constructed two new engines in 1902.

The railway serving the By-Products Works was much smaller and far less complex than that which operated in the gas works itself. The premises lay to the north-west of the site and adjoined the southern bank of the Northern Outfall Sewer.

The purpose of this plant was to refine the various by-products which resulted from gas manufacture and therefore make them suitable for further use. Amongst these commodities were tar and pitch.

Processing commenced in 1879 and for a number of years the factory was known as The Tar & Liquor Works.

Although both owned by the same company, the two establishments were regarded as being totally separate, as indeed were their internal railways. The locomotive stud which operated around the By-Products Works was numbered in a completely different sequence, and comprised only fifteen engines.

98. Here we see the main signal box on the high level lines, which controlled operations in and around the retort houses, as well as a junction where a double-track formation diverged to circumnavigate the entire site. It was equipped with around 60 levers and displayed an impressive array of block instruments, together with a large track diagram. There were two other signal boxes on the high level section, both of which were equipped with 44 levers. (J.E. Connor Collection)

99. The main purpose of the high level lines was initially to transport coal from riverside piers to the retort houses. After leaving the piers, the tracks crossed the river wall, then ran between the retort houses for around 1,200 yards. At this point there were six parallel tracks, two on what was known as the central viaduct, and the others on either side, passing through the retort houses themselves. This view illustrates the scene perfectly, and includes an incline linking the two levels on the right. All in all, the system had three of these, with gradients which ranged from 1 in 30 to 1 in 40. (London Gas Museum)

100. The low level lines covered virtually all of the works area. They had various purposes, including the collection of coke from the retort houses, and taking it to a grading plant near the river. Some of this would end up fuelling the works' boiler houses, although the majority was sold for outside consumption. Apart from this, they were also used for the transportation of other by-products and general equipment around the site, and provided access to the locomotive depot and workshops. Here, 0-4-0T No 24, constructed by Neilsons in 1896 and subsequently rebuilt at Beckton in 1930, is seen prior to setting off from beneath a huge coal bunker with a full load of coal, which is destined for the high level lines and retort houses. (London Gas Museum)

101. This is the impressive interior of Beckton locomotive works, with various engines undergoing repair. In the early years of the twentieth century, the locomotive and wagon shops employed around 600 men. All engineering work for the internal railway system was carried out here including repairs to locomotives, wagons, signalling and permanent way. It comprised three lathe shops, two smiths shops, two gas-fitters shops, a boiler shop, a pattern shop, a foundry, a carpenters shop, a tinsmiths shop, a coppersmith shop, an iron wagon repair shed and a wooden wagon repair shed. (London Gas Museum)

102. Here we see one of the signal boxes which controlled the low level tracks, together with a neatly planted avenue of trees to the right, which somehow seem a little out of place! (J.E. Connor Collection)

103.   The locomotives employed at Beckton largely comprised 0-4-0 side and saddle tanks, which were built to very squat dimensions so that they could work safely within the confines of the works. Here one of the saddle tanks is busy shunting three dead engines outside the depot's roundhouse in the 1950s. These saddle tanks, which were mostly constructed by Neilson & Co of Glasgow between 1883 and 1896, were built to the extremely small loading gauge of 6ft 6ins, so that they could pass through the ground level retort house entrances. For some reason, they were nick-named 'Jumbos'. (RAS Marketing)

104. Judging from this photograph, the locomotive running sheds must have been very sulphurous places to work! The engines employed in the main gas works were finished in apple green, lined out in white and black, whilst their coupling rods were painted red. (London Gas Museum)

105. Similar lining was employed on the locomotives working in the By-Products Works, although in this case, the basic livery was maroon. Here engine No 1 is seen nicely posed in the 1950s. Diesel locomotives began to replace steam at Beckton during 1958 and 59, although an 0-4-0T was retained until March 1967 to keep the last retort house in operation. With the general conversion to Natural Gas, the huge works became redundant and production ceased on 16th June 1969. Complete closure followed within a few years, and eventually the demolition gangs moved in. (RAS Marketing)

3. Gallions Branch

106. To obtain this view, it is thought that the photographer was standing on a signal post. He was looking east towards Albert Dock Junction and recorded the Beckton branch diverging on the left and the 1855 route to Silvertown, together with its later deviation in cut-and-cover tunnel on the right. In the centre however is the line which we will now follow, namely the 'Royal Albert Dock Passenger and Parcels Railway', or as it was commonly known, the Gallions Branch. This was owned and staffed by successive dock companies, but for the majority of its life, services were provided by the GER and LNER. The first station was named Connaught Road, and this can be seen shortly beyond the junction to the right of the signal box. (British Rail / D. Brennand Collection)

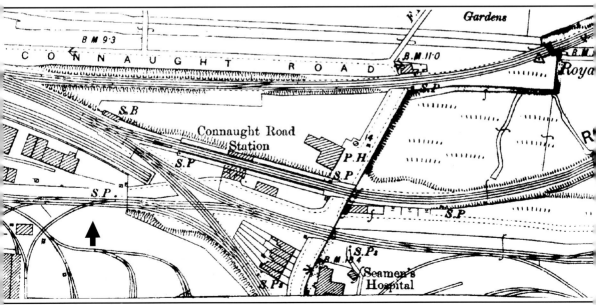

Albert Dock Junction and Connaught Road station are shown on this Ordnance Survey map of 1894, together with some of the internal dock lines near the bottom.

CONNAUGHT ROAD

107. Opened on 3rd August 1880, Connaught Road station exhibited a strange mix of Swiss chalet and Mock-Tudor styles. This 1930s view looks across to the entrance, which was incorporated into the main building, located on the up side. (Lens of Sutton)

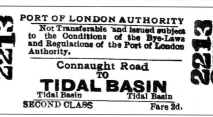

PORT OF LONDON AUTHORITY
Not Transferable and issued subject to the Conditions of the Bye-Laws and Regulations of the Port of London Authority,

Connaught Road
TO
TIDAL BASIN
Tidal Basin   Tidal Basin
SECOND CLASS   Fare 2d.

2213   2213

108. Connaught Road was well-used by dockers travelling to and from their place of work, as seen here in the 1930s. The photograph was taken from the footbridge and looks west. The inclusion of the word 'Station' on the platform nameboard to the left is unusual, although not unique. (Stations UK)

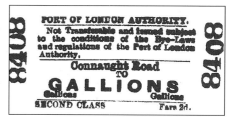

PORT OF LONDON AUTHORITY.
Not Transferable and issued subject to the conditions of the Bye-Laws and regulations of the Port of London Authority,

Connaught Road
TO
GALLIONS
Gallions   Gallions
SECOND CLASS   Fare 2d.

8408   8408

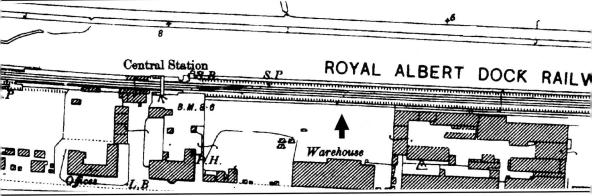

This station received its wonderfully ambiguous name because its was positioned approximately mid-way along the Albert Dock estate. When opened on 3rd August 1880, it was used as a temporary terminus, as the remainder of the branch into Gallions was not quite ready at the time. As can be seen from the Ordnance Survey map of 1894, there was little in the way of housing in the immediate vicinity, and its chief means of access was from the dock itself, which lay immediately to the south. Central station was reduced in status to a halt around 1933, although whether staff were retained or not is uncertain.

109. Central was virtually identical in styling to Connaught Road, with its main building again on the up side, and a footbridge at its eastern end. Initially the route between Connaught Road and Central comprised a single line, but the formation subsequently doubled, with the second track being approved by the Board of Trade on 14th November 1881. (Stations UK)

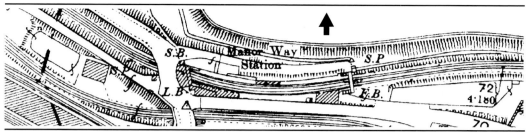

Opened as Manor Road in July 1881, the station stood on the west side of what later became East Ham Manor Way. Its name was changed to Manor Way about a year after opening, but other than this little is known about it. Following changes at Gallions terminus, which resulted from nearby dock alterations, Manor Way was resited to the opposite side of the road around 1887 and the old premises were totally demolished. This Ordnance Survey map shows the layout as it appeared in 1894. The line between Central and Gallions was single until 1st April 1882, when a second track was brought into use.

110. This is the street level building of the 1887 station, viewed from the west side of Manor Way itself. At one time there seems to have been an additional ticket issuing facility at platform level, as tickets are known which include the legend 'Lower Office', although evidence of this is very scant. As can be seen, the signal box was curiously tucked away against the parapet, but was seemingly constructed high enough to allow the signalman a clear view of the track on the opposite side of the bridge. The road was widened in 1926, and the street level building shown here was replaced by a new structure of more utilitarian appearance. (Newham Local History Library)

111. The alterations of 1926 are not thought to have resulted in any substantial changes at platform level, although by the 1930s, when this photograph was taken, the signal box had disappeared. Here, we are looking west, as a former GER 2-4-2T, carrying an 'Albert Dock' destination board, enters with a Fenchurch Street-Gallions train. (Stations UK)

G. E. R.

Manor Road

(ROYAL ALBERT DOCK)

---

112. The Gallions branch closed from 8th September 1940 following air-raid damage, but Manor Way's 1926 street level building survived into the late 1970s, having been adapted for non-railway purposes. This view shows it shortly before demolition. (J.E. Connor)

113. Abandonment of the Gallions branch was officially sanctioned by Section 29 of the Port of London Act 1950, and although the tracks were retained for wagon storage, they had gone by the time this photograph was taken in 1967. As can be seen, the up platform survived, but its wooden counterpart on the down side had gone without trace. (J.E. Connor)

114. This view, dating from the autumn of 1969, looks east towards the end of the up platform, where there was once a footbridge and a small building, *possibly* the erstwhile "Lower" ticket office referred to earlier. The station site has since been largely buried, leaving just an upper section of retaining wall above ground level, but the Gallions Hotel, visible in the mist, has been granted Grade ll listed status. (J.E. Connor)

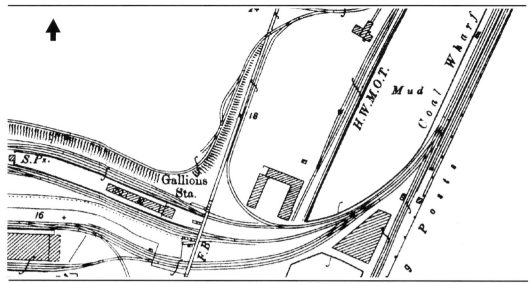

The original Gallions station, which opened in the autumn of 1880, was resited 275 yards further east on 12th December 1886, when the line had to be diverted slightly to facilitate dock alterations. The new premises consisted of an island platform, which is shown here on the Ordnance Survey map of 1894. Beyond Gallions, the tracks continued towards the river, and served a coal wharf and jetty which was subsequently leased to the firm of Cory Brothers.

115. The Gallions Hotel was built to serve the needs of ship passengers, and adjoined the north side of the original branch terminus. After this closed, part of its platform was retained and adapted as an open raised area in front of the hotel, which was used as a public house until January 1972. Similar buildings, designed by Messrs. George Vigers and T.R. Wagstaff, were erected to serve the stations at Connaught Road and Central, and all three remained standing in 2000. (H.C. Casserley)

116. To operate its passenger services, the dock company acquired three 2-4-0Ts from the London & North Western Railway, all of which had been rebuilt from 2-4-0 tender locomotives. This is No 7, which had started life as LNWR No 431 *Hercules*. She was recorded around 1890, standing at the southern face of Gallions island platform, whilst waiting to depart with a train for Custom House. This face of the island was dubbed platform 2 and was generally used exclusively by local services, whilst the northern face, or No 1 as it was known, was dedicated to Great Eastern trains. There seems to have been doubt as to the presentation of the station's name in early days, as in addition to the generally accepted spelling, it was sometimes shown as "Galleons", "Galleon", or in the case of the 1880 Board of Trade inspection report, "Gallions Reach". (J.E. Connor Collection)

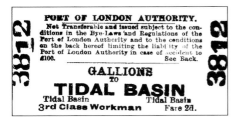

117. Around 1925 the original building was demolished and replaced by a smaller one. This 1930s view looks west from the footbridge which provided access to the station and includes a GER train standing at Platform 1. (Stations UK)

118. Although taken from a less-than-perfect print, this view has been included as photographs featuring moving trains on the Gallions branch are incredibly rare. It shows a Class N7 0-6-2T arriving with a passenger train at Platform 2, whilst a 2-4-2T awaits on the adjoining track to take the stock back out on its return working. Part of the Gallions Hotel is visible behind the locomotive, although this has unfortunately been 'touched-in' by an artist, presumably because it was indistinct on the original negative. The local service between Gallions and Custom House was withdrawn in 1932, leaving just the through trains to and from central London. (J.E. Connor Collection)

119. The branch closed in September 1940 and Gallions remained largely intact for a few years after. The building was still standing in the early 1950s, but had gone by 1965, when this view was taken looking west. The concrete section of platform visible in the foreground is believed to have dated from the 1920s. (J.E. Connor)

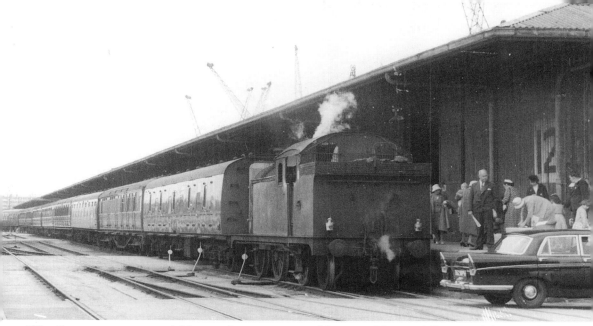

120. For many years, special boat trains were operated between Liverpool Street and the Royal Albert Dock. These ran by way of the Stratford Western Curve, and took the 1855 route beyond Custom House. They travelled over part of the internal dock railway, as opposed to the Gallions branch, which no longer functioned after September 1940. This view dates from August 1961 and shows a grubby Class N7 0-6-2T standing beside Shed No 12, after arrival at King George V Dock. (B.P. Pask)

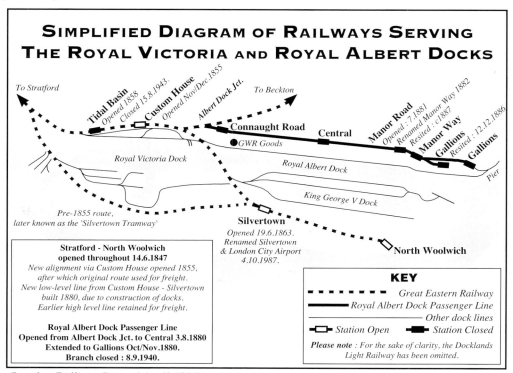

SIMPLIFIED DIAGRAM OF RAILWAYS SERVING THE ROYAL VICTORIA AND ROYAL ALBERT DOCKS

To Stratford

Tidal Basin *Opened 1858 Closed 15.8.1943.*

Custom House *Opened Nov/Dec.1855*

Albert Dock Jct.

To Beckton

Connaught Road

● GWR Goods

Central

Manor Road *Opened : 7.1881 Renamed Manor Way 1882 Resited : c1887*

Manor Way

Gallions *Resited : 12.12.1886*

Gallions

Pier

Royal Victoria Dock

Royal Albert Dock

King George V Dock

Pre-1855 route, later known as the 'Silvertown Tramway'

Silvertown *Opened 19.6.1863. Renamed Silvertown & London City Airport 4.10.1987.*

North Woolwich

Stratford - North Woolwich opened throughout 14.6.1847
New alignment via Custom House opened 1855, after which original route used for freight. New low-level line from Custom House - Silvertown built 1880, due to construction of docks. Earlier high level line retained for freight.

Royal Albert Dock Passenger Line Opened from Albert Dock Jct. to Central 3.8.1880 Extended to Gallions Oct/Nov.1880. Branch closed : 8.9.1940.

KEY

━ ━ ━ ━ ━ *Great Eastern Railway*
────── *Royal Albert Dock Passenger Line*
────── *Other dock lines*
◻— Station Open   ◆— Station Closed

***Please note** : For the sake of clarity, the Docklands Light Railway has been omitted.*

(London Railway Record April 1995)

MP Middleton Press

Easebourne Lane, Midhurst, W Sussex. GU29 9AZ Tel: 01730 813169 Fax: 01730 812601
If books are not available from your local transport stockist, order direct with cheque,
Visa or Mastercard, post free UK.

BRANCH LINES
Branch Line to Allhallows
Branch Line to Alton
Branch Lines around Ascot
Branch Line to Ashburton
Branch Lines around Bodmin
Branch Line to Bude
Branch Lines around Canterbury
Branch Lines around Chard & Yeovil
Branch Line to Cheddar
Branch Lines around Cromer
Branch Lines to East Grinstead
Branch Lines of East London
Branch Lines to Effingham Junction
Branch Lines around Exmouth
Branch Line to Fairford
Branch Lines around Gosport
Branch Line to Hawkhurst
Branch Lines to Horsham
Branch Lines around Huntingdon
Branch Line to Ilfracombe
Branch Line to Kingswear
Branch Lines to Launceston & Princetown
Branch Lines to Longmoor
Branch Line to Looe
Branch Line to Lyme Regis
Branch Lines around March
Branch Lines around Midhurst
Branch Line to Minehead
Branch Line to Moretonhampstead
Branch Lines around North Woolwich
Branch Line to Padstow
Branch Lines around Plymouth
Branch Lines to Seaton and Sidmouth
Branch Line to Selsey
Branch Lines around Sheerness
Branch Line to Shrewsbury
Branch Line to Swanage *updated*
Branch Line to Tenterden
Branch Lines around Tiverton
Branch Lines to Torrington
Branch Lines to Tunbridge Wells
Branch Line to Upwell
Branch Lines of West London
Branch Lines around Weymouth
Branch Lines around Wisbech

NARROW GAUGE
Branch Line to Lynton
Branch Lines around Portmadoc 1923-46
Branch Lines around Porthmadog 1954-94
Branch Line to Southwold
Douglas to Port Erin
Kent Narrow Gauge
Two-Foot Gauge Survivors
Romneyrail
Southern France Narrow Gauge
Vivarais Narrow Gauge

SOUTH COAST RAILWAYS
Ashford to Dover
Bournemouth to Weymouth
Brighton to Eastbourne
Brighton to Worthing
Dover to Ramsgate
Eastbourne to Hastings
Hastings to Ashford
Portsmouth to Southampton
Southampton to Bournemouth

SOUTHERN MAIN LINES
Basingstoke to Salisbury
Bromley South to Rochester
Crawley to Littlehampton
Dartford to Sittingbourne
East Croydon to Three Bridges
Epsom to Horsham
Exeter to Barnstaple
Exeter to Tavistock
Faversham to Dover

London Bridge to East Croydon
Orpington to Tonbridge
Tonbridge to Hastings
Salisbury to Yeovil
Swanley to Ashford
Tavistock to Plymouth
Victoria to Bromley South
Victoria to East Croydon
Waterloo to Windsor
Waterloo to Woking
Woking to Portsmouth
Woking to Southampton
Yeovil to Exeter

EASTERN MAIN LINES
Ely to Kings Lynn
Fenchurch Street to Barking
Ipswich to Saxmundham
Liverpool Street to Ilford

WESTERN MAIN LINES
Ealing to Slough
Exeter to Newton Abbot
Newton Abbot to Plymouth
Paddington to Ealing
Plymouth to St. Austell
Slough to Newbury

COUNTRY RAILWAY ROUTES
Andover to Southampton
Bath Green Park to Bristol
Bath to Evercreech Junction
Bournemouth to Evercreech Jn.
Cheltenham to Andover
Croydon to East Grinstead
Didcot to Winchester
East Kent Light Railway
Fareham to Salisbury
Frome to Bristol
Guildford to Redhill
Reading to Basingstoke
Reading to Guildford
Redhill to Ashford
Salisbury to Westbury
Stratford upon Avon to Cheltenham
Strood to Paddock Wood
Taunton to Barnstaple
Wenford Bridge to Fowey
Westbury to Bath
Woking to Alton
Yeovil to Dorchester

GREAT RAILWAY ERAS
Ashford from Steam to Eurostar
Clapham Junction 50 years of change
Festiniog in the Fifties
Festiniog in the Sixties
Isle of Wight Lines 50 years of change
Railways to Victory 1944-46
SECR Centenary album
Talyllyn 50 years of change
Yeovil 50 years of change

LONDON SUBURBAN RAILWAYS
Caterham and Tattenham Corner
Charing Cross to Dartford
Clapham Jn. to Beckenham Jn.
Crystal Palace (HL) & Catford Loop
East London Line
Finsbury Park to Alexandra Palace
Kingston and Hounslow Loops
Lewisham to Dartford
Lines around Wimbledon
London Bridge to Addiscombe
Mitcham Junction Lines
North London Line
South London Line
West Croydon to Epsom
West London Line

London Suburban Railway continued .....
Willesden Junction to Richmond
Wimbledon to Beckenham
Wimbledon to Epsom

STEAMING THROUGH
Steaming through Cornwall
Steaming through the Isle of Wight
Steaming through Kent
Steaming through West Hants
Steaming through West Sussex

TRAMWAY CLASSICS
Aldgate & Stepney Tramways
Barnet & Finchley Tramways
Bath Tramways
Bournemouth & Poole Tramways
Brighton's Tramways
Burton & Ashby Tramways
Camberwell & W.Norwood Tramways
Clapham & Streatham Tramways
Croydon's Tramways
Dover's Tramways
East Ham & West Ham Tramways
Edgware and Willesden Tramways
Eltham & Woolwich Tramways
Embankment & Waterloo Tramways
Enfield & Wood Green Tramways
Exeter & Taunton Tramways
Greenwich & Dartford Tramways
Hammersmith & Hounslow Tramways
Hampstead & Highgate Tramways
Hastings Tramways
Holborn & Finsbury Tramways
Ilford & Barking Tramways
Kingston & Wimbledon Tramways
Lewisham & Catford Tramways
Liverpool Tramways 1. Eastern Routes
Liverpool Tramways 2. Southern Routes
Liverpool Tramways 3. Northern Routes
Maidstone & Chatham Tramways
Margate to Ramsgate
North Kent Tramways
Norwich Tramways
Portsmouth's Tramways
Reading Tramways
Seaton & Eastbourne Tramways
Shepherds Bush & Uxbridge Tramways
Southampton Tramways
Southend-on-sea Tramways
Southwark & Deptford Tramways
Stamford Hill Tramways
Twickenham & Kingston Tramways
Victoria & Lambeth Tramways
Waltham Cross & Edmonton Tramways
Walthamstow & Leyton Tramways
Wandsworth & Battersea Tramways

TROLLEYBUS CLASSICS
Croydon Trolleybuses
Bournemouth Trolleybuses
Hastings Trolleybuses
Maidstone Trolleybuses
Reading Trolleybuses
Woolwich & Dartford Trolleybuses

WATERWAY ALBUMS
Kent and East Sussex Waterways
London to Portsmouth Waterway
Surrey Waterways
West Sussex Waterways

MILITARY BOOKS
Battle over Portsmouth
Battle over Sussex 1940
Bombers over Sussex 1943-45
Bognor at War
Military Defence of West Sussex
Military Signals from the South Coast
Secret Sussex Resistance
Surrey Home Guard
Sussex Home Guard

OTHER RAILWAY BOOKS
Garraway Father & Son
Index to all Middleton Press stations
Industrial Railways of the South-East
South Eastern & Chatham Railways
London Chatham & Dover Railway
War on the Line (SR 1939-45)